## DATE DUE

| | | | |
|---|---|---|---|
| | | | |
| | | | |
| | | | |
| | | | |
| | | | |
| | | | |
| | | | |
| | | | |
| | | | |
| | | | |
| | | | |
| | | | |
| | | | |
| | | | |
| | | | |
| | | | |
| | | | |
| | | | |
| | | | |
| | | | |
| GAYLORD | | | PRINTED IN U.S.A. |

# SERENADING LOUIE

10 $^{00}$

# SERENADING
# LOUIE by Lanford Wilson

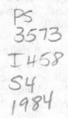 *HILL & WANG NEW YORK*

*A Division of Farrar, Straus & Giroux, Inc.*

SERENADING LOUIE was first presented at the
Washington Theater Club in Washington, D.C. on April
1, 1970. The cast was as follows:

MARY    *Anne Lynn*
CARL    *Arlen Dean Snyder*
GABBY   *Jane Singer*
ALEX    *Robert Darnell*

*Directed by*   Davey Marlin-Jones
*Setting and Costumes by*   James Parker
*Lighting Design by*   William Eggleston
*Production Stage Manager*   Robert H. Leonard

*SERENADING LOUIE* was presented by The Circle Repertory Company in New York City on May 5, 1976. The cast was as follows:

MARY      *Tanya Berezin*
CARL      *Edward J. Moore*
GABBY     *Trish Hawkins*
ALEX      *Michael Storm*

    *Directed by*  Marshall W. Mason
    *Setting by*  John Lee Beatty
    *Costumes by*  Jennifer Von Mayrhauser
    *Lighting by*  Dennis Parichy
    *Production Stage Manager*  Dave Clow

*SERENADING LOUIE* was presented by The Second Stage in New York City on January 17, 1984. The cast was as follows:

MARY    *Lindsay Crouse*
CARL    *Jimmie Ray Weeks*
GABBY   *Dianne Wiest*
ALEX    *Peter Weller*

*Directed by*  John Tillinger
*Setting by*  Loren Sherman
*Costumes by*  Clifford Capone
*Lighting by*  Richard Nelson
*Production Stage Manager*  Kate Hancock

# SERENADING LOUIE

We will serenade our Louie
While life and voice shall last
Then we'll pass and be forgotten with the rest.

(The Whiffenpoof Song)

## CHARACTERS

CARL        Ex-quarterback, maybe a martini
            overweight, warm, introspective.

MARY        His wife, ex-homecoming queen,
            from conservative and wealthy fam-
            ily; breeding everywhere.

ALEX        Fast becoming a public hero; boyish,
            entertaining, shrewd.

GABRIELLE   The only one not a graduate of
            Northwestern, she's from Stevens;
            not dithery, her situation is dithery.

All are around thirty-four.

# ACT ONE

*The present. Early evening.*

*The living room of a suburban home, north of Chicago.*

*A door to a kitchen, through which is the garage, at least one set of French doors leading to an outside area, a window seat, and a door to the master bedroom. Stairs up to the child's room. Spacious and expensive, modern or traditional, American antique furniture, eighteenth or early nineteenth century and good.*

*This one set, which should look like a home, not a unit set, will serve as the home of first one couple, then the other, with no alterations between.*

*Lighting from actual source, or the illusion of such. The divisions between scenes in the first act should be marked with an abrupt blackout. At the end of the scene, blackness, followed by lights up full in as short a time as possible—no more than, say, ten seconds.*

## Scene 1

*Nearly evening. The only light is on the desk.*

CARL: *(Coming from the kitchen as he closes the out-side door, he calls from offstage)* Sweetheart? *(He enters)* Honey? . . . Mary? *(He yells up the stairs)* Hey, baby? *(He goes to the patio door, yells out)* Mary?

*He shuts the door, turns, and sees the light—he goes to the desk, picks up a note, and sits as he reads it. He lets the note float from his hand back to the desk, shuts his eyes a moment, reaches to the desk lamp, and turns it off.*

*(Blackout)*

## Scene 2

*(Gabrielle, a.k.a. Gabby, is asleep in a chair, a book in her lap. She awakens as Alex comes in the front door.)*

GABRIELLE: Hello, baby; I didn't realize . . .

*(Alex looks to the living room; seeing her, he shows the barest recognition. He leaves his topcoat in the foyer closet, and as she talks he comes to the sofa, bringing his briefcase)*

GABRIELLE: Have you read this? It isn't . . . well, I don't know what it isn't. Like a drink? What kind of day?

*(A pause. Alex crosses to the desk to pick up the mail)*

GABRIELLE: I was in town and going to stop by or call, and then just got too tired. Claris wanted to call it a day too. She's really . . . oh, I don't want to say anything, I suppose we all are, but she really is. More and more. You know I went back to bed and slept till almost ten-thirty. I thought pot wasn't supposed to give you a hangover. Maybe I'm just getting something. You slept terribly, perspiring all . . . I think I enjoyed last night; you seemed to. Carl's fun, isn't he? Of course Mary's great. I kept thinking *(Enjoying this)* that my head was going to . . . leave my . . . you know, with pot I've decided that it changes the focus of my eyes. I see things at a distance more clearly. Or something. I don't know, it's very funny. *(She leaves for the kitchen)*

ALEX: Any moment now you'll hear a woman talking to a roast.

GABRIELLE: *(From the kitchen, to Alex)* I heard a joke. There was this . . . no, I won't, I'll call Mary and get it straight. I always mess them up.

*(Alex goes to the foyer closet, gets his cigarettes from his coat pocket, comes back, picks up his briefcase, and sits at a chair with a lamp beside. He opens his briefcase. Noises are heard from the kitchen—the oven door, etc.)*

GABRIELLE: I think I've *(Reenters, crossing to the sofa)* got a really good roast for a change. It's getting cool, isn't it? *(She drifts to the window where she sits after a moment, looking out)* I used to love the autumn so much. Oh God, I *(Thinking of an amusing story, laughing a little to herself)* remember one time on the way . . . you know, it had frosted and I had a little purse—it must have been the first grade, and I picked up this leaf. This bright red leaf because it looked . . . there was a frost . . . a thick rime covering it—and I put it in my purse to give to the teacher to tack up on the bulletin board because it was . . . I thought it was so lovely. *(She laughs, quite to herself. Smiles. Looks out the window)* Up through Thanksgiving I love it. Brisk . . . crisp. Bitey. Astringent. The Farrenstein's sugar maple looks like it's on fire—did you see it?

*(She thinks about something, laughs to herself . . . a "humph" sound, twice. Perhaps she thinks about a Halloween experience; perhaps she says a very dear, "Oh," as in, "Oh, dear, how silly of us," and then looks outside again, smiling. A sigh.)*

GABRIELLE: I want to remember to ask Alison when it is you cut back delphiniums . . . she's incredibly knowledgeable on . . . I've probably already . . . *(She starts to go somewhere, has a new impulse, turns)* I don't think kids now . . . oh, maybe they do . . . I don't think they enjoy Halloween as much as we did. Why don't we get a jack-o'-lantern? I'd love that. I'll make some pies . . . that isn't silly, is it? *(She ducks into the kitchen again, speaks from offstage)* Aren't you cute . . . Very good. Actually I think you could use a little . . . no, that's *(The oven door closes; she comes back)* lookin' pretty good, huh!

*(She sits at the desk, looks to Alex. She smiles, watching him concentrate on his work. She tilts her head to the side. Count twelve before he looks up)*

ALEX: *(Rather like, "What, darling, I'm sorry, but I'm busy.")* What is it?

GABRIELLE: Nothing, I just like to watch you working.

ALEX: *(Lighting a cigarette)* Humph. *(He looks back to his work)*

GABRIELLE: *(Moving toward the phone)* I should call Alison and ask her. I think she said October or the

first of November . . . I should remember, Mother
. . . *(Seeing a note by the phone)* Oh, Mrs. Porter
called and said . . . what is it? Look at page fourteen
of the *Sun-Times* . . . did you see that? *Sun-Times*,
page . . .

ALEX: Yeah, it was nothing.

GABRIELLE: *(Crossing to the sofa)* Is that some explo-
sively scandalous disclosure for tomorrow? I thought
we were finished with all that. *(Pause. He continues
without acknowledgement)* I know better than to ask
if I've done something, don't I?

*(Alex looks up. Beat)*

GABRIELLE: Or haven't done something.

*(Alex goes back to his work)*

GABRIELLE: It isn't going to be one of those "silent"
nights, is it? Working all night silently and then going
to work and calling me five times to talk about nothing as though you hadn't been silent? I don't much
like those nights, but I rather enjoy the phone calls.
Or aren't we supposed to talk about it? *(Beat)* Would
that impede your spontaneity? *(Beat, as he doesn't
react)* It wouldn't.

*(Alex looks at her directly. She holds his gaze. Count
five. He shakes his head, looks back to his papers)*

GABRIELLE: It doesn't . . . *(Suddenly she thinks of the roast)* Did I? No, I did. *(She moves to the sofa, picks up her book)* Actually, I'm enjoying this. I mean it's nothing . . . you know.

*(She sets the book on her lap, opens it, settles down, begins to read. Alex clears his throat. She looks up smiling and back. He stacks some papers, lays them aside. Rather dramatically he stubs out his cigarette. Looking to her, he shakes his head. She continues to read)*

ALEX: *(Going into the bedroom)* I guess I should know by now, shouldn't I?

GABRIELLE: What's that, honey? *(She looks up, not certain where he has gone. Calling toward the bedroom)* Baby? What'd you say, hon'? *(She listens)* Honey? *(After a second, getting up, crossing to hall, calling)* Alex?

ALEX: *(Off)* What, for God's sake?

GABRIELLE: Nothing. I wondered . . . where . . .

ALEX: *(Off)* I'm going to lie down.

GABRIELLE: Really? Honey, you . . .

ALEX: *(Off)* What?

GABRIELLE: Nothing, only you spend . . . and dinner's just . . .

ALEX:  *(Off)* All right, I won't lie down; it doesn't *(Reentering, he crosses to the desk)* matter to me, I'll work, it doesn't matter.

*(He turns on the lamp, sits, and reopens his briefcase, looking through his papers)*

GABRIELLE:  It's just that when you're home you spend every waking hour asleep. Of course, you're never home.

ALEX:  I'm not asleep, Gabrielle.

GABRIELLE:  Well, awake then; it's worse if anything. I know your eyelids like the back of my hand. If I lie down beside you, you get up. You look in pain if I sit on the side of the bed to talk to you anymore. Oh, I'm sorry, you must be exhausted . . . don't work . . . if you're tired, of course you should lie down.

ALEX:  I'm not tired.

GABRIELLE:  Would you like a drink? Before dinner? Alex? Would you like . . .

ALEX:  *(Making a notation, interrupting, preoccupied)* No, thank you, hon'.

*(Pause. She goes into the kitchen. Alex looks up to the door. There are noises in the kitchen. Alex lights a cigarette. Watching, thinking. He looks to the floor. She reenters. Alex goes back to staring through the papers, smoking. She walks over to him, behind his chair)*

GABRIELLE: Is that a speech? Are you . . .

ALEX: No, I just never seem to get to this.

GABRIELLE: What's that?

ALEX: Nothing, it's nothing.

GABRIELLE: I'm looking very fondly toward you going back to trial cases. The cold-blooded murders I can understand—all that dirty politics and under-the-table graft and deals is all so . . . Dinner's on the brink. You hungry?

ALEX: I'm not very, actually.

*(He continues to work. She smiles, walks to the window, looks out)*

GABRIELLE: It's getting dark earlier and earlier. Pretty soon . . . *(She turns on the living room light. She smiles to Alex. Then a thought crosses her mind and she frowns.)* Do we know a man with white hair? We don't know many older people, do we? A very . . . well, not quite distinguished-looking man, but nearly. I think he's . . . following me.

ALEX: Where?

GABRIELLE: Well . . . I know, isn't it? But in town I thought I saw him . . . then, when I came out of the Safeway. He was in a car watching me . . . but really *watching* me. And across the street from the

florist. I ran to the car; then he followed me in his car
and drove on by when I turned in the drive. I suppose
I imagined it? I mean, what could he want, right?
During the hearings I would have been really fright-
ened, but now that it's all over—well, I get so jumpy
at every little thing lately. I feel so inse . . . Oh, it's
silly, isn't it? *(Pause)* I don't know how to react to
these moods you get into lately. *(Pause)* I . . .
*(Pause)* Well, there isn't someone else, is there, Alex?

*(Alex turns to her)*

GABRIELLE: Doesn't that sound silly, but I can't come
up with . . . It's driving me nuts, and that's all I can
come up with. I won't care . . . honestly . . . well,
maybe I'll care, but I won't do anything; I just wanted
to ask, it's been on my mind.

ALEX: No, Gabby. There isn't. I really, well—

*(He goes back to his work, quite irritated)*

GABRIELLE: I didn't know, I thought maybe . . . I
. . . I have your report memorized almost. The summation I think I could actually quote verbatim. I
thought it was brilliant. Ponderholtz must be spitting
nails . . . I've been so . . . Oh, I'll be quiet. I know.
I'm being silly . . . so many things . . . I'm sorry. I
guess I'm just nervous tonight. It's silly. I was with
Mary yesterday. For some reason, she decided to be
confiding. I don't know why me. I suppose she
thought . . . Poor Mary. She's having an affair. Did
you know that? I don't know if you know him. He's

very good-looking. We saw them on the street; they
have three kids . . . girls too. His wife's very attrac-
tive . . . I couldn't imagine. Apparently they're in
love. Of course they both have the children. It just
makes me nervous. I wish she hadn't told me. I hate
secrets.

*(Alex stares at her. A pause)*

GABRIELLE: Did you know anything about it?

ALEX: I thought it was possible.

GABRIELLE: Does Carl know?

ALEX: How would I know?

*(Pause. Gabrielle crosses to the window seat)*

GABRIELLE: I wouldn't do that to Carl. He scares me
sometimes. He's so . . . trusting . . . He's too . . .
something. I wouldn't want to . . . What do you
think?

ALEX: *(not unkind)* I think you're overreacting.

GABRIELLE: So what's new? *(Sits)* They finally sold that
summer cabin up on Lake Elizabeth.

ALEX: Good, they hadn't been there in years.

GABRIELLE: Well, Lake Elizabeth isn't what it used to
be.

ALEX: What is?

GABRIELLE: *(Looking down into the window. A laugh)* Oh, there's a little fly . . . a drunk fly here. Turning fall, isn't it, old boy! He can't *(She passes a fanning hand at it)* even fly off. *(She is struck by a remembered line of something)* Oh, what is . . . ? "Flat upon your bellies—where the . . ." What . . . how does . . . ? "Where the fuzzy flies are crawling . . . buzzing . . . crawling . . . By the webby window lie. Watch the . . . Read me . . ." Or "young lovers by the . . ." *(She thinks a moment)* I can't, I can't . . . I've no idea. Silly, anyway. How's it coming?

*(Alex continues to work. After a second she looks outside, then back)*

GABRIELLE: Alison's sister is . . . well, I don't think you know her. *(Pause)* Alex? *(No answer. More urgently)* Alex? *(After a second)* I don't want to—

*(Gabrielle smiles and looks down, out the window, a hand to her face. She begins to cry. Alex, without looking at her, puts his work aside, stubs out the cigarette, and gets up, walking briskly to the closet. Frantically Gabrielle wipes her cheeks, running after him)*

GABRIELLE: I'm sorry, honey, I can't imagine! Alex? It's just . . . I'm sorry, Alex. Come on.

*(Alex has taken his coat from the closet, throws it on, reaches for the front door)*

GABRIELLE: Alex, where . . . Baby, I don't know what's wrong . . . *(Laughing)* I think I must be . . . Baby, please don't go! Alex!

*(Alex slams the door on her last word, and with the sound the lights go out)*

*(Blackout)*

## Scene 3

*(Early evening. Carl is standing in the middle of the room. Mary enters from the bedroom, carrying her shoes. She is getting dressed, will put on the shoes, belt, scarf, etc. during the scene)*

MARY: Gabby scares me. I don't know if she scares me or if she's freaking out and imagining it: someone keeps following her.

CARL: Man or woman?

MARY: Oh, she's a very sweet girl. You should indulge her sometimes. She's scared.

CARL: I just asked if it was a man or woman.

*(Carl crosses to Mary to zip her dress)*

MARY: A man but not like that. Oldish, very distinguished, she thought. Very unlike a rapist. *(Carl has slipped his arms around her)* Is your watch right? I've got to split. Hat, gloves, purse, shoes, what?

CARL: Keys, list . . .

MARY: What list?

CARL: Did you have a list?

MARY: No list.

CARL: Umbrella?

MARY: It wouldn't dare. Purse, scarf, shoes, gloves, keys, no list . . .

*(Carl crosses to the closet and gets Mary's coat)*

CARL: I thought it was a party for someone's birth . . .

MARY: *(Crosses to the desk)* Right! Right . . . present! Thank God, that's all I'd need.

*(Mary takes it from the desk, putting it into her purse. Carl follows to the desk)*

MARY: Present. Keys in purse. Pencil for bridge scores . . . Anyone else we'd make it during the week, but Sue works. If you'd let me know you weren't going in today. Now, you're not going to forget to pick up Ellie at five-forty. She hates walking home carrying her ballet slippers.

CARL: Check.

MARY: She loves the class; she just doesn't like the school. Take her night bag, drop her at Bunny's, I've got her PJ's and all her paraphernalia already in it.

CARL: I know, I know.

MARY: And you'll remember to turn off the oven when the bell rings.

CARL: *(In a thicker mood than she)* I'll not forget.

MARY: Chicken pot pie; it's no good burned. You're going to forget, aren't you?

CARL: *(Smiling)* No, no, what's to forget. The bell rings, turn off the oven.

MARY: There's bologna and cheese in the fridge if you forget. It should be time by now.

CARL: You're going to pick up Sue?

MARY: Sue and Alice; I'm late, you're right.

*(Mary crosses to the front door)*

CARL: *(Frowning; reluctantly)* Honey, I'd like to . . .

*(Carl halts, looking to her. She looks to him. All movement and sound are arrested for a count of fifteen)*

MARY: *(A rapid, overlapping exchange now)* What, doll?

CARL: Talk, you know.

MARY: I know . . . we will. Nothing's wrong is there?

*(Mary crosses to the living room)*

CARL: No, no.

MARY: With that Atlanta business?

CARL: No, no.

MARY: *(Still lightly)* What is it?

CARL: No, no, it's nothing.

MARY: We're running all over, we're never home together, I know . . .

CARL: It's nothing, Mary, I just get . . . edgy . . . it'll pass.

MARY: *(She crosses to Carl, maneuvering him to the sofa)* I know, baby. It'll pass. *(She sits, smiling)* Sit a second.

CARL: It's OK, no, it'll . . .

MARY: Sit a second. *(She pulls him down to sit beside her, relaxes)*

CARL: No, I never know when I'm going to be here; even Ellie, with her new schedule . . .

MARY: Oh, but she loves it . . .

CARL: No, no, I think it's great. She's a little lady . . . a little goddess.

MARY: I don't think Ellie would respond well to being worshipped. I know I wouldn't.

CARL: Sure you do.

MARY: Do you like the shadow puppet?

CARL: Yeah. He's cute; it's cute.

MARY: A little fierce, but I thought he was amusing. He's about a thousand years old . . . well, old in any case, they said. He's parchment.

CARL: They had puppet shows back then? And we think we're so advanced.

MARY: I wouldn't think they'd be much like ours. I mean it's not Punch and Judy. I think it's more closely related to religious stories, like for children, but not just . . .

CARL: Bible school.

MARY: Well, it wouldn't be "Bible." Their equivalent . . . "Bhagavad-Gita Illustrated" or whatever. *Bible school?* Did you do that?

CARL: *(Laughing)* No, I don't think I managed . . . that was summertime; would have interfered with softball practice, but Sunday School . . . I went to that every Sunday, bright and early. Well, nine o'clock.

MARY: I can't imagine. What did you do?

CARL: What did . . .

MARY: What was it like? Did you like it?

CARL: Oh, yeah . . . I liked . . . Well, there wasn't any question of not liking . . . it was this thing you did. We, ah . . . what was it . . . ? We all had these . . . our own . . . little pulp-paper quarterlies— thin little magazines that we were taught from—with orange and black illustrations of young Jesus, aged eleven, in the temple astonishing the . . .

MARY: Whoever. Right . . .

CARL: And we were taught by the judge's daughter or his son or some such, and they were seventeen, probably, and knew all the Psalms by heart. Especially the twenty-third. "Valley of the shadow of death, I will fear no evil for Thou art with me. Thy rod and Thy staff, they comfort me . . ." *(He sighs. Mary is polite attention personified)* Oh, God . . . and uh . . .

when it was someone's birthday . . . their ninth or
tenth, we sang: "Ebert's had a birthday, we're so
glad. Let us see how many he has had."

*(Mary, charmed, has been laughing at this)*

MARY: Oh, that's wonderful. *Ebert?*

CARL: Well, I just picked Ebert at random. There were
some pretty incredible names. We had a boy named
Dillard and twin girls called Ima Daisy and Ura
Pansy . . .

MARY: Ura Pansy . . . no . . . nobody would saddle a
kid with . . .

CARL: Swear to God. Ima Daisy and Ura Pansy Mag-
gart. That kinda ruins it, doesn't it?

MARY: How can you remember that? How do you remember that tune?

CARL: How do you forget it? I learned it before "Happy
Birthday to You." And Ebert had brought pennies
and he dropped them into this round cardboard
Quaker Oats box with that very severe Quaker in this
flat hat . . . and the pennies hit the bottom and
bounced like dropping on a drum. Or it might have
been—that's funny—a milk bottle with tin foil over
the cap—I remember them both—and in that case
they jingled around in the glass. *(Beat)* I can hear
them both. Anyway, as Ebert . . .

MARY: *(Laughing)* Ebert.

CARL: Well, or Dillard. We sang, "How old are you?" and Dillard dropped his pennies and we all counted. One. Two. Three. Four. Five. Up to eight or nine, or sometimes very dramatically, "Ten!" and we all . . . you know, the boys . . . watched those nine years go into the bottle and longed to be twenty-one and have a draft card . . .

MARY: I can't imagine . . .

CARL: Or at least sixteen and have our driver's license, and my Aunt Grace used to say, "Don't wish your life away." Then when the teacher, the mayor's daughter, or sheriff's son, had a birthday, he played too and . . .

MARY: Of course.

CARL: . . . and that was an Event that lasted forever because he had to drop eighteen drumming pennies into that—

MARY: Or the other . . . the milk bottle.

CARL: Right. And it seemed to last half the Sunday School period.

MARY: I'm sure.

CARL: That was an Event . . . kids came from the other classrooms to watch. Everything was an Event then. The smallest thing that happened was an Event.

MARY: Of course.

CARL: And we don't have those anymore. Why is that? What's happened? *(He slides from his mood, back closer to his first one)*

MARY: *(Still quizzical)* What?

CARL: I don't know. That wars and deaths, birthdays, Easter, even Christmas. Nothing gets to me like that now. *(A slight pause)* Things go by and nothing reaches us, does it? Nothing's an Event anymore.

MARY: Ummm. *(Pause. She jingles the keys)*

CARL: *(More or less coming out of it for her benefit)* You've got to go.

MARY: Oh, I know. *(Getting up)* Now, I'm not going to tell you about the pie again—if it burns, there's bologna and cheese.

CARL: Turn off the oven; pick up Ellie at five-forty. Take her overnight bag . . . Drop her at Bunny's.

MARY: You'll be all right. Can we go out tomorrow night? Would you like that? I think I would. Just us?

CARL: Great. Saturday night . . .

MARY: Dinner and maybe a movie . . . I'd like that . . . we can call Betty to stay with Ellen. OK? I'd love that.

CARL: It's a deal.

MARY: OK, now, I've got to run. If the girls call, tell them I've left. *(She kisses him on the top of the head)* OK?

CARL: OK. Right.

MARY: *(Opening the door)* Bye-bye, sweetheart.

CARL: Bye-bye.

*(Mary leaves. Carl crosses to the sofa, his smile fades, he looks down to the floor with a worried look; after a count of ten, he looks up to the audience with a sense of urgency. The buzzer sounds in the kitchen, offstage. Carl turns his head to the sound)*

*(Blackout)*


## Scene 4

*(Alex holds a large clipping from the newspaper. The silent TV has a football game on. Carl enters from the kitchen with a tray of sandwiches and beer)*

ALEX: Hey, Bozo, who's the war hero, one of your buddies?

CARL: Isn't Mary something else? I'll bet I haven't mentioned that guy more than five times. She recognized him and cut that out so I'd see it. I told you about him, the guy with the camera; sent Mary a picture of me reading one of her letters—sitting on the can. The way they razzed me about her, I had to go into the latrine—the only place I could read my mail in peace.

ALEX: *(Regarding the TV)* Who's playing?

CARL: It's nothing. It's a rerun of an old Super Bowl game. *(Carl turns off the TV)* Saw your mug on the news again today. You really kicked against the pricks.

ALEX: Yeah, they wanted an interview . . . a summary of my committee summation . . . apparently unable to sum it up themselves . . . wait till Monday.

CARL: I thought it was over.

ALEX: *(Gets sandwich)* Wait till Monday, completely different thing.

CARL: What are you into now?

ALEX: Watch Monday.

CARL: Tell me.

ALEX: Better not right now. Wait till it's official.

CARL: No, better tell me now. I have to be in Cincinnati Monday. I have to see some people about an office building.

ALEX: Carl, you're going to be the youngest dead millionaire I know . . .

CARL: Have you ever heard me say I liked it? Running around like this? I don't go more than I have to—it's not my money; it's the bank's money, the investors' money.

ALEX: What's in Cincinnati?

CARL: It's nothing—an office building, in Oakwood. You know, suburban doctors' offices, dentists—that kind of thing. Half finished.

ALEX: They've run out of financing?

CARL: Money is what they've run out of. Tell me about your thing Monday.

ALEX: They have papers in Cincinnati.

CARL: Oh, great, you bastard, you're going to start giving me hints. I'd know if I'd been following it. I read up on you when I can . . . Christ, my hands are dry.

Goddamn humidifier. Mary waters the plants three times a day.

*(Carl crosses to the thermostat)*

ALEX: *(He bites something in the sandwich, reacts)* Jesus, wow.

CARL: What is it? Bite your tongue?

ALEX: *(Pointing to his mouth)* Tooth. Damn. *(He manages to swallow, breathe, and then throws his sandwich back on his plate)* I never seem to make it to the damn dentist.

CARL: Looks like you'd better. What is it, tender?

ALEX: Tender hell, it's gone. Oh, Jesus. "For the want of a nail the shoe was lost"—right? Sometimes I can't believe it . . . everywhere I look it's falling apart. I'm winding up the hearings last week . . . on my feet . . . I feel like I'm sweating . . . I think, Lord, I'm really worked up . . . I look down and my ink pen's leaking all down the front of my shirt . . . inside my jacket. Fourteen cameras on me, I'm ripping Ponderholtz's defense apart . . . brilliantly.

CARL: I'll bet.

ALEX: All I'm thinking is it's soaked through to my skin; I'm standing there like Napoleon. I start leaving fingerprints all over the table.

CARL: Nobody saw it?

ALEX: How do I know? No, just me. Had to wait till recess to change my shirt. Had to take a shower. Elastic on my shorts was blue. Aww, it's always something—my grandfather's pen, too. Beautiful old Waterman . . . you couldn't buy one like it. I had it in school . . . holds about a gallon of ink—all down my —oh, Jesus, Carl, I keep feeling my real life will begin any day now. This can't be it. This is just temporary. A dry run. I have a whole agenda of tabled activities. I've got two temporary fillings I've had for a year and a half. They're wearing away a little bit everyday. I can feel it with my tongue. My mother keeps calling me collect—to tell me to write her more often. I have my girl send her clippings—she writes me to get a haircut; you look too thin; I bet you eat nothing but sandwiches. Everything is tabled till next meeting.

CARL: Waiting for someday when the taxes go down and you get the mortgage paid off.

ALEX: I have to discuss this total upheaval with Gabby; I've known for a week and a half.

CARL: That's the Monday thing. What total upheaval?

ALEX: Did I say that? Forget I said it.

CARL: I'm going to figure it out and I'm going to kick your ass.

ALEX: Trouble is, the other day I had a flash of objectivity and made the mistake of asking myself what I wanted to do with my life. You're better off to go at it blind. You take it all in, and it all begins to look . . .

CARL: And it all falls apart—I know the feeling.

ALEX: Never do that—ask what it's all about. Never do that. *(He gets a sandwich)* What do you want to do with it? I'll tell you exactly what I'd like to do with it.

CARL: Don't eat that if you're going to get a toothache.

ALEX: No, it's stopped. My thirty-fourth birthday I stood in the yard and looked down the block. This came as quite a revelation to me. I said, Alexander, you are not going to alter the course of the planet in any way. You aren't going to be President, or change the course of law, or eliminate injustice or graft to any tangible extent because you can bellow about corruption from the steeple of the First Presbyterian Church, but all the guys down the block are burning leaves. What they're *doing* with their *lives* is *burning leaves*.

CARL: How do you know?

ALEX: Know what?

CARL: That that's what they're doing. They may be writing to their mother more often and going to their dentist, telling the wife about Monday's upheaval.

ALEX: Carl, where's it getting them? What are they *doing?* They're *burning leaves.*

CARL: All right and burning leaves. It's important to them to have leaves burned. You like a sloppy lawn. Don't knock them for cleaning up.

ALEX: Paying bills, fighting with Gabby, pains in my leg, firing the secretary, heartburn. That's just not what it's all about. I begin to see the sense of following the call of Maxey Gene Connell and flying to Ibiza. Law buddy of mine . . . Phi Beta Kappa . . . valedictorian, Ph.D. in chemistry on the side. Tending artichokes and wild strawberries on the sunny hill of an island off Spain. Now it's going to take a great deal of talking to convince me he's got the wrong idea.

CARL: As big a hypochondriac as you are? Where would you find a dentist?

ALEX: No, it's stopped, it's fine.

CARL: Alex, life is a ballbreaker, it really is. Twenty percent of the people in the country are on dope, twenty percent of France is wiped out on wine twenty-four hours a day. It's too much for them. They can't take it. They can't take life, man. I don't blame them. It's a mess. When I was a kid, I had it all worked out. The whole point was to be happy. I was going to write a book . . . "The Principle of Life," I was going to call it.

ALEX: Modestly.

CARL: Well, goddamnit, I wasn't wrong! Of course I
didn't have any principles except you should go to
church on Sunday and be kind to dumb animals. And
work sounded like play; I didn't know it was work.

ALEX: You were also single, which doesn't hurt.

CARL: No, that's different, that's the only good thing in
all of it. I just thought it would be all very simple.
"Building," "developing" were terrific words. I
didn't think it'd take business managers and advisors
and accountants and lawyers and investors, and
everytime you wanted to do something as simple as
plant a tree you couldn't get a hold of the landscap-
er's accountant's secretary. I didn't know you had to
get ahead; hell, I thought you could just lope along.

ALEX: You've managed to get pretty well ahead.

CARL: In the beginning it was fun; hell, it was a ball
game. But people aren't prepared if you just want to
play fair. It amazes me. The whole country's profi-
teering and pickpocketing each other; it's a daisy
chain. That's what business amounts to. We're all telling each other every minute how important all the
things we believe in are, how the world would col-
lapse if we let up for a minute believing all the things
we believe and doing all the things we do and, hell,
nobody believes it. We all know it's a shell game. It
strains all our faculties keeping all the lies straight
and juggling all the rationalizations and pretending

we don't notice everyone struggling with it, and you tell me you're not contented with your lot. Jesus Christ, Alex, it's a lousy lot . . . nobody's content with it. Hell, I know what it is; of course that's what it is!

ALEX: What what is?

CARL: Monday. Your Monday thing. The commission thing, right?

ALEX: I don't know . . . what?

CARL: Okay. You've just investigated a scandal involving the Department of Transportation and City Funding, right?

ALEX: Right.

CARL: And the recommendations in your summation stressed the need for a department to handle private funding where the income was derived from a broad cross section of the people.

ALEX: More or less, I thought you didn't follow it.

CARL: Everyone followed it generally; I didn't follow it all that close.

ALEX: I'm not above an occasional generalization.

CARL: And the city is going to have to accept the idea or have it rammed down their throats.

ALEX: That was our intention, yes.

CARL: And the new department is going to have to have someone to head it—who should be brave and loyal and kind and honest and . . .

ALEX: Loyal, brave, fearless, kind, honest, and true. That's not it.

CARL: Not what?

ALEX: That's not Monday.

CARL: For real.

ALEX: That's not it.

CARL: Better than that.

ALEX: Maybe.

CARL: Bigger.

ALEX: Might be.

CARL: You're really a prick, you know that?

ALEX: *(He crosses to the desk)* You'd know what it was if you read the paper.

CARL: I'm not interested anymore. How come you haven't told Gabby? If it's so great for you, such an upheaval . . . Well, don't look like that. How come you haven't told her?

ALEX: Because if I told her I'd have to talk to her, and I can't talk to her. You should hear our conversations, or what pass for conversations. Actually long, analytical examinations of the day's minutiae. Why I didn't call seven times to tell her I'd be late . . . or why I *did*, if you can believe it. She wants me back on trial cases which are a dead end, but she knows when to expect me home for dinner. I say, honey don't expect me till late. So she doesn't expect me till six or seven. I get home at ten, she's crawling the walls. I say, honey, don't *expect!* If we'd have to sell the house . . . or lease it.

CARL: Sell the house?

ALEX: Or lease it or something. If . . . maybe. Aw, hell, she wouldn't even hate that. She goes along with anything. Gabby would go along with it if we had to move into the county jail. She'd be in there polishing and scrubbing. She's probably all the penal system really needs.

CARL: Gabby's all right.

ALEX: No, Carl, it isn't a joke. She's changed. She's not really happy, she's compulsive. She used to relax. I'm apparently no good for her at all; nothing's right about it. Even sex. Brother, I really turn off sometimes. I'd just like to get a good night's rest. I go to bed and manage to get to sleep and she wakes me up.

Only gently, always gently as if that made it all right.
She keeps at it till she manages to turn me off altogether. And she can't even see what she's doing . . .
apparently never notices the effect of a thing she
does. Every time I do turn on to her, she tells me she's
deliberately turned off to see if I'll come around—so I
come around and she starts that "Oh, I know you so
well" routine. She's playing little secret intrigues
with me. It's ridiculous; I don't enjoy it. Being raped.
Every night. By my own wife. What kind of married
life is that?

CARL: I wouldn't know. I don't have that kind of problem . . .

ALEX: You think men are sex-conscious. It's them . . .
only the girls in our generation are so damned over-
sexed, by the time they get married you give them a
lifetime guarantee and they wear you out in the first
six weeks. Girls should start getting screwed at about
age nine and a half; then maybe they'd lose some of
their illusions about it. They think that's the only way
they can make their husbands happy. Gabby could
make me most happy by going home to Mother for a
month. I understand. I finally understand why men
have children when they don't really want them,
can't afford them, don't want them—they think
maybe something two feet long and that big around
stuffed up there for a couple of months day and night
will finally satisfy them and they can get some sleep.

CARL: (Enjoying him) I wish to hell I'd made it down to
the hearings to see you at work. You're great. No

wonder you're getting famous. You are the best irrelevant spitballer in town. You don't believe anything you say. Look how you work yourself up. That's beautiful.

ALEX: I never say anything I don't believe.

CARL: But you can believe anything. You believe it as you say it. No joke, you walk into the courtroom and they applaud. Like for a film star. An entertainer. They eat you up.

ALEX: Just for the record, I think we should make it clear that in school this football star, and hero . . .

CARL: *(Over)* OK, OK, enough . . .

ALEX: Millionaire construction developer magnate, jock, minored in Nineteenth-Century Romance Lit.

CARL: OK.

ALEX: Damned near switched to teaching.

CARL: Probably should have.

ALEX: You think I don't believe that? I know men who for a fact have got their wives pregnant just because they were becoming exhausted with . . .

CARL: *(Overlapping a good deal)* Don't start again, what do I know about it?

ALEX: Maybe that's why a girl wants it. So she'll get pregnant. I mean, finally. Maybe that's why they're so compulsive, without even being aware of being compulsive. We might be dealing with some psychological truth here. Maybe they can't even help it.

CARL: Maybe you're just undersexed.

ALEX: No, I'm not under . . .

CARL: Wait. It isn't that, is it?

ALEX: What? Undersexed?

CARL: Did someone die?

ALEX: When?

CARL: You're not talking about Old Man Hayes? Representative Hayes, dying six days after being reelected to something like his fiftieth term in the House; keeled over flat on Michigan Avenue. The Governor has to appoint a replacement to fill Hayes's term. Is that an *(Crossing to the fireplace)* appointment or do we have a special election?

ALEX: No, no, no, no. It's a special election. But the Governor does hand-pick the nominee.

CARL: So, call it an appointment.

ALEX: Call it an appointment. *(A long pause. Carl looks a little troubled, confused)* And?

CARL: No, I think it's fine for the Governor and the Mayor and the Commissioner of Transportation. It's so logical and glamorous and popular. It's the obvious move. Hell, why wouldn't Gabby go along with it if that's what you want. Is it?

ALEX: I said I'd consider it.

CARL: Oh, sure. *(Troubled pause)* I know you really do have very definite feelings under all the . . . It's just not what I expected.

ALEX: Well, listen. I'll be going. I want to thank you for the toothache.

CARL: No, wait a minute. Is that what you want? Politics?

ALEX: I said I'd think about it.

CARL: You wouldn't have to sell your house or rent it. You'll only be gone for two years.

*(Alex reacts)*

CARL: Oh, hell. You get to Washington, you'll never come back. You'll be President.

ALEX: If I knew you were going to be so happy for me . . .

CARL: You're a natural . . .

ALEX: I can't discuss it now . . .

CARL: OK, OK . . . of course not. You know damn well if you want it, I want you to have it. What's with Gabby now? Why isn't that working? What's antagonizing things?

ALEX: I don't want to discuss it; it's fine . . .

CARL: You look happy enough to me—when I see you, the two of you . . . you're the perfect couple.

ALEX: I'm happy. I'm OK. I feel great! I don't know why! Of course we look happy to you. We go out and she's fine. We have a ball. We get home and she changes completely. Her voice changes, the way she walks changes, she stops laughing, or she starts laughing seductively.

CARL: He's off again.

ALEX: It's like she has a little movie of the evening up in her head and we've come to the X-rated scene. You should see the array of nightgowns she's got. She must think I've got a fetish. Or maybe she has. Why should it only be men who have fetishes? Outside with you and Mary she's fine. She comes home with just me and she changes completely. I love her too . . . out. I could fuck her under the table. We get home and she practically turns to oatmeal on the threshold. She loses every bone in her body. I have to hold her up. Her kisses all turn to tongue. Like she was trying to get me hot. Hell, I was hot already. If I don't bang her in the pachysandra, she's going to turn me off by the time I can get my pants unzipped.

CARL: Your problem is you don't like big sloppy kisses. Other guys I could name live for big sloppy kisses. Some people think big and sloppy is the only way to kiss. Every book you read, "She melted into his arms with her mouth moist and open . . ."

ALEX: I don't know what books you've been reading lately.

CARL: You're making a big issue out of what is basically a matter of taste. I'd say offhand that you didn't love her, but I don't want to hear it.

ALEX: No, not that. Well. Less and less. You don't love someone all the time. You love them for moments. A while now and a while after a while. And with Gabby the times are getting fewer and—all right—you like to get me going. Prove my lack of convictions. Get me going. I'm sorry to be such a drag-ass, kvetching about my problems when your business is in such good shape, your married life is on such solid rock, so idyllic—and so . . .

CARL: I didn't say that. Don't start in on me now.

ALEX: The one good island in a shit-soup of disillusions.

CARL: Come on.

ALEX: Carl, you're completely transparent. Never play poker, Carl; you're going to lose your shirt.

CARL: We're not at your hearings, Alex; you're not on the House floor. Don't cross-examine me.

ALEX: Then what is it? You're turning all wooly and introspective. Morbidly thumbing over your . . .

CARL: I haven't felt well.

ALEX: You're a physical horse, Carl. Mentally, the species is somewhat different lately.

CARL: I've had headaches for the past . . .

ALEX: I don't know how you can tell a hangover from a headache in the condition you're usually in.

CARL: Alex, I'm not interested in being the subject of one of your tirades.

ALEX: Hell's bells and goddamn, Carl; you know she's cheating on you, don't you?

CARL: You son of a bitch!

ALEX: Don't you?

*(A long pause)*

CARL: Does everybody know?

ALEX: I don't think so. Gabby told me.

CARL: She isn't a whore . . . I think she really loves him . . . it isn't like that.

ALEX: Did she tell you?

CARL: No, she doesn't know I know. I don't imagine. I saw them once. Well, I knew before that. I mean, it's something you know. There uh . . . "there needs no ghost," you know? "Come from the grave to tell me this . . ."

ALEX: Yeah, yeah, I know, got it.

CARL: He has a family too. Three girls.

ALEX: You know who he is?

CARL: Oh, sure . . . no, skip it. This isn't any good. It's no big deal. It's a comedy . . . it's a farce; it's not to be serious about.

ALEX: But you know who he is?

CARL: Yes. He's my CPA. See? His firm does the accounts for my office. Now, no more. I don't think about it. It's all the same to me.

ALEX: Mary is a powerhouse, Carl, you've got to keep ahead of her . . . Hell, you know that. You used to be ahead of things.

CARL: At least you didn't say I got to keep on top of her.

ALEX: What are you doing? Joking? What are you doing?

CARL: Alex, I see it like I see everything else—like I'm up in the air and it's down on the ground happening to someone else. It doesn't affect me. Nothing, now . . . shut up about it. Please.

ALEX: OK.

CARL: I am doing nothing. To my surprise. Nothing. Waiting.

ALEX: Floating.

CARL: Waiting. It'll burn out. My God, we've been married nine years; it's normal. It's no big deal. I envy your energy that you can be concerned. It isn't just Mary; Alex, I'm sorry. I can't get involved with anything. What did you call me, "wooly"?

ALEX: No, no.

CARL: "Wooly" is perfectly fair. But I'm sorry, even as you're going on about Gabby and you, I keep thinking—I mean, I love you very much—but if it came to the worst, you'd split up and she'd get the house and alimony and you'd get Washington and the car. And besides, I know it won't come to that. I can't imagine you taking old silent Hayes's seat in the House because I can't imagine anything. I come home and I

read what you've been saying and watch the
roundup of the day's news events and all that's happening in the world and it seems like a lot is, but I
don't follow it. I watch and hope along that something will involve me. Touch me. Grab me. Piss me
off. Something. Involve. It's the same thing as with
Mary. I can't galvanize any concern. Nothing anyone
says is real—how am I supposed to relate to it? Involve. I have an office manager who boils over . . .
gets worked up over . . . I remember, when I was
. . . You'll remember . . . everyone remembers
. . . I don't know when it was . . . twelve years ago
or more . . . I was a kid. No, I was only about twelve
or so, so it was longer ago than that. Somewhere in
Colorado or Ohio or Wyoming or somewhere in the
world a little girl was playing in her backyard or near
a mine shaft or somewhere, and the ground caved in
or she got too close to the well, but she fell down, way
down—forty or seventy feet or so into a hole. I don't
know where it was, but this little girl was in this hole
in the ground. She was about three years old or five or
something like that. And they couldn't reach her, and
firemen came and men with various kinds of gear—
and they were afraid of caving in the sides of the hole,
and they tried to dig her . . . reach her . . . dig her
out. They could hear her and knew she was alive.
And everyone all over the country stayed around
their radios and prayed for her. And telegrammed
the parents' hope and messages of compassion and
love and hope for this little girl. It was like a war, it
was like a kidnapping or like that. A whole country—
the whole world—people twenty thousand miles

away—were alarmed and concerned for this one
. . . one . . . one girl. Little girl. This little kid.

*(A long pause)*

ALEX: And what? *(Beat)* What happened?

CARL: *(Looking at Alex)* Huh? You don't remember
that? I thought everyone would remem . . . No, I
didn't mean it like . . . It isn't a story or something.
It happened. That wasn't what I meant . . . I remember she died before they could reach her, but
that wasn't why I . . . I didn't tell it to be sad. I just
think of that time as a time when people were involved. Those events where the whole world goes
into suspension and holds its breath at once, and for a
little while comes together in something they realize
is in some way, more important—significant—than
anything else at that moment. Some crisis. Some danger. *(A wondering, brief pause)* We've gotten much
too civilized for our own good, Alex. And I wonder
. . . at times . . . what . . . the pagans . . . the
primitive people . . . how they felt after a public
sacrifice. There's a need, some need, somewhere, for
that important . . . contribution. So many people
feel compelled to sacrifice themselves in one way or
another, excuse or another, cause or another. Themselves or something very dear. Or expose it to danger. *(He sits)* I try to understand her. Mary. I try to
understand that she needs for some reason to expose
our marriage to danger. That she needs the danger
more than she needs whoever it is . . . more than
she wants anything with Donald. Not sacrifice it if

possible, but expose it to danger, herself, our marriage, Ellen. But then probably I just want to think that because I don't like believing that she loves someone else more than she does . . . It's usually the man's place to have the affair, isn't it? I thought that was our downfall.

*(Beat)*

ALEX: From the last statistics I read I understand it takes two.

CARL: Maybe I'm just naive about that. Ironic thing, of course, being she's safe really, because I can't for the life of me seem to get involved in being betrayed. Even by someone I love so . . . well, you know. Because like everything else for the last two years or so it just doesn't seem worthwhile, Al. Alex. Alexander. It happens to someone else. Of course you're tied up into things, various concerns, you're . . .

ALEX: Oh, hell, yes. I have concerns out the ass. The government, birth control, the aged, the starving, the homeless and the shiftless, the useless . . .

CARL: Yeah. Well, I see it and I try to say all the things I feel, express my concerns, but deep down I'm not fooling myself because I know that really . . . honestly . . . at bottom . . . I don't care. I don't care. I envy you that you can, but I just don't care. I don't care. Care. C-A-R-E.

ALEX: I know how to spell it. I see it on "El" posters.

CARL: When's the last time you were on the train?

ALEX: A lot. Really. I go. All the time. Never mind. Skip it.

CARL: They make love in the afternoon, for God's sake. When they can get away. We never did that, even before we got married. When I was getting my degree. She was a morning repeater. But not afternoons. She never liked to. Does Gabby?

*(Carl gets a drink)*

ALEX: Oh, come on, Carl.

CARL: No, no lie, does she? Gabby? If you don't mind . . .

ALEX: You can't learn it by the books. Your experience is not my experience, my experience isn't yours. It isn't even Gabby's experience! Sure. Sometimes. Given Gabby. We have. She loves it!

CARL: *(Suddenly)* Cathy Fiscus. Was the little girl's name. Little Cathy Fiscus.

ALEX: *(Looks to him, smiles. A pause)* In the afternoons, yeah, sure. Afterwards . . . should we go out . . . among people . . . Saturday afternoon, Sunday. I feel . . . well, like I've had it. Castrated. Shot. And I don't mean it funny or clever—spent. Oh God, now you'll go to work or get on the phone, someone'll ask you what you did you'll say, oh . . . spent the

whole goddamned weekend hearing this story about
a castrating female or about this guy who felt castrated . . . but try to see what I mean, past all this,
what really is . . . for me . . . or for you . . . or
Gabby. I mean walking with her, if we've made love
in the afternoon, and go out, sometimes I get really
mad at her for having robbed me of something. It's
like I'm "safe" now. I feel like I'm this temporary
eunuch in her . . . power. It's nothing strong, and
it's only in the back of my mind, fizzing away back
there where it's worse . . . But I get furious with
her. I'd just like to be reassured that I wasn't the
world's only man who felt cut, gelded—after sleeping
with his own wife. Ravaged . . . I'd like just once,
dear God take me back to the good old eras past, just
once like to ravage her! I wish to hell it was Gabby
who was . . . You don't know how easy you have it.

CARL: Sure, right.

ALEX: You'll never have that delicious feeling of being
in service.

CARL: You know I don't agree with any of your . . . I
always feel very proud . . .

ALEX: Hell, you don't know how good you've got it.
Mary plays around with your accountant and you stay
home . . .

CARL: Come on . . .

ALEX: . . . crocheting a goddamned afghan or something.

*(Carl slugs Alex quite hard—and immediately, with a
cry, grabs hold of Alex's shoulders—holding him
tightly)*

CARL: Alex, Alex. I do! I do! I try to understand and see
what's going on, and I see it all go by sometimes like a
movie. But I try to understand why she needs this or
how it happened and because I rattle on about it I
think it doesn't move me any more than anything
else . . . Alex, why does she have to do it?

*(Alex, taken completely off stride, is trying to answer,
trying to comfort, but neither is possible)*

CARL: *(Shouting)* WHAT'S SHE TRYING TO DO? I
DON'T KNOW WHAT TO SAY. I DON'T KNOW
HOW TO FEEL, ALEX. I DON'T KNOW HOW
TO FEEL. I WANT IT BACK—LIKE IT WAS. IT
WAS GOOD THEN.

*(Flooding. Alex, over, can mumble, "What, Carl,
what?")*

CARL: IT WAS GOOD THEN, GODDAMNIT,
WHEN I WAS OVER THERE—OVERSEAS—
AND WE WROTE LETTERS TO EACH
OTHER; IT WAS GOOD THEN, IT WAS GOOD
THEN. IT WAS GOOD! IT WAS!

*(Blackout)*

## Scene 5

*(After midnight. The silent TV shows only snow; the only light in the room. Gabrielle opens the bedroom door. Standing in the light of the door, in her nightgown, holding a pillow in her arms)*

GABRIELLE: Alex? Are you here? Alex?

ALEX: Yes.

GABRIELLE: Were you asleep?

ALEX: No, that's all right.

*(Alex turns off the TV. The only light comes from the bedroom door)*

GABRIELLE: Honey . . . ?

ALEX: Oh, God.

GABRIELLE: What's wrong?

ALEX: When you get into that tone of voice and say honey like that, I know we're up for the night.

GABRIELLE: No, we aren't . . . I . . .

*(Pause)*

ALEX: What, Gabby? *(Pause)* What, I'm sorry.

GABRIELLE: Nothing. What can I say? . . . Nothing . . . *(goes back to the bedroom, closing the door)*

ALEX: I said I'm sorry.

*(He openes up the door, stands there)*

GABRIELLE: No, nothing.

ALEX: Gabby? *(Pause)* Gabby, baby, I'm sorry, what? *(Pause)* Gabby?

*(He goes to the bedroom, closing the door. Blackout)*

*(Curtain)*

# ACT TWO

*Night. The room is brilliantly lit around the bar area. Mary and Alex are talking to Gabrielle, quite spirited, laughing; lines tumble over each other.*

ALEX: And we're jammed-packed into someone's god-awful claptrap of a . . .

MARY: Eddie Bender's god-awful Pontiac . . .

ALEX: Eddie Bender's Pontiac. All bellowing these sing-along songs at the top of our lungs, we're sliding all over the road, we've got about six dozen oranges in a shopping bag . . .

MARY: *(Completely over)* Oh, God, yes, I'd forgotten all about the oranges . . .

ALEX: . . . down around our feet with two ounces of Vodka shot into each . . .

MARY: Yes, because the faculty frowned on us passing the flask at games.

GABRIELLE: Oh, God, oh, how . . .

ALEX: Right, right . . .

MARY: They didn't mind us drinking, they frowned on us passing the flask.

ALEX: We get to the game to see Carl who was like the most important quarterback in the history of the Big Ten.

GABRIELLE: *(Completely over)* I know, I know.

MARY: *(Over)* He really was, you know.

ALEX: And by the half we didn't even know who we were playing.

GABRIELLE: Who spiked the oranges?

MARY: Who knows?

ALEX: One of the pre-med bunch, with a syringe.

MARY: I'll bet he went far.

ALEX: And for some reason Bender almost never drove his own car and you have . . .

MARY: I don't think he even had a license.

ALEX: *(Without stopping)* . . . no idea who's driving or who's sitting on your lap, but her hair's in your face and mouth and all the windows are open and there's a wind flying through the car . . .

MARY: Bitter cold—November.

ALEX: . . . and everything smells of leaf smoke and wool sweaters and the oranges and leather . . .

MARY: Old Spice aftershave and cigarettes and we're all bundled up in blankets and quilts . . .

*(Carl enters, his collar turned up)*

MARY: Hello, darling. You get Betty home all right?

CARL: Yeah.

MARY: It's getting cold, isn't it?

CARL: *(Putting the keys in a bowl)* Warm in the car.

ALEX: And Bozo always took bass. He wasn't bass, but he took the counter stuff . . .

MARY: Because he couldn't carry a . . .

ALEX: Hey, Bozo! *(Singing)* "You throw a silver dollar down upon the ground and it'll roll—because . . ." Come on! "And it'll roll . . . because . . ." Come on, that was your part . . .

*(Carl has just come into the room, still with his coat on, as he will remain throughout the scene. His arms are slack, rather troubled, not at all in their tempo)*

CARL: I don't . . .

ALEX: You flubbed your part. You took bass.

CARL: I don't remember, not on that one . . .

MARY: You remember that, honey, sure you do.

ALEX: Sure you do.

ALEX AND MARY: "A woman never knows what a good
man she's got, until she turns him . . . down, down,
down, down"—you mean to tell me you honestly
don't remember . . . ?

MARY: Everybody knows that.

ALEX: That one?

CARL: (Crossing to the steps to Ellie's room, troubled,
unheard) Ah, guys, would you mind terribly . . .

| ALEX: | MARY: |
|---|---|
| I think he only remem-<br>bered the . . . | Everyone excepting Carl<br>was bombed. |

GABRIELLE: Well, he had to play.

MARY: Speaking of pleasantly high, how come you
haven't any grass this week? Where do you get it,
anyway?

ALEX: I'll never tell.

GABRIELLE: He won't even tell me.

MARY: One of your future constituents has a backyard plot. Well, that will never do. Why don't I mix up something strong for a cold night.

CARL: *(Crossing to the dining room)* Sure.

MARY: Something quasi-exotic like a sidecar. And we'll toast our new congressman.

ALEX: I haven't said I'd take it; I'm thinking. We're thinking, aren't we, darlin'?

GABRIELLE: *(To Alex)* Hadn't we better go soon? It's incredibly late.

MARY: No, it isn't bad. On a cold night like this and after that movie I think a sidecar sounds conservative.

CARL: *(To Alex)* I was probably worrying about the game and not singing any . . .

ALEX: You worry? Are you kidding? He didn't have a nerve in his body.

MARY: Did you remember to pay Betty?

CARL: Yeah.

MARY: I hope she isn't coming down with something. Ellen catches anything communicable within twenty miles. She looked dreadful.

CARL: *(Crossing into the entry, he gets a mask)* She said she had a toothache.

MARY: Oh, God. Has she seen a dentist?

*(Alex groans)*

MARY: That's the most horrible pain.

GABRIELLE: None for me, love.

MARY: Sure you will.

ALEX: Come on, a nightcap.

GABRIELLE: I'm half asleep already.

MARY: *(To Gabrielle)* You didn't know the Northwestern campus did you? I keep forgetting.

ALEX: It used to be beautiful. Really lovely.

MARY: Before the landfill.

GABRIELLE: I can't say I like it now.

MARY: Oh, it's a crime, but it used to be marvelous. Carl, would you stop playing with that—what is that you're playing with?

CARL: You guys see this? *(Picking up the mask of a bull)* I got it at the—*(Holding the mask to his face)* Moooooooooo!

GABRIELLE: No. No. Carl! Oh, that's terrible.

CARL: You don't like it?

GABRIELLE: Oh, God.

CARL: I liked it. They're plastic. They had incredible masks this year.

MARY: Remember when plastic was going to save the world?

GABRIELLE: No, I love it, no, it's great, but not a cow! Why a cow?

CARL: That's not a cow. That's a bull!

MARY: Carl was a bull and Ellen was a calf; he took her trick-or-treating around the . . .

GABRIELLE: Oh, how great . . .

ALEX: You should have asked Gabby to come along . . .

GABRIELLE: Yes, I'd have loved it.

CARL: I was a smash in all the living rooms on the North Shore.

MARY: *(She gives Carl a drink)* Darling, you were smashed in all the living rooms on the North Shore.

CARL: That too, that too . . .

MARY: They cleaned up. Didn't you see the dish of knosh in the hall?

CARL: That's me. I'm Taurus. The Bull. It's a bull.

MARY: *(Pouring and passing drinks)* Darling, you're Scorpio, you're not Taurus. I'm Taurus.

CARL: Really?

MARY: You know that; your moon's in Taurus.

CARL: *(He gives the mask to Mary)* Well, you should have it then. Here.

ALEX: Or you could wear it on your moon.

CARL: That'd be a neat trick.

MARY: *(Dryly)* Wouldn't it.

*(They sip their drinks)*

GABRIELLE: Ummmm. Lemon juice, brandy, and . . . triple sec?

MARY: Cointreau.

GABRIELLE: Ummmm. Cointreau.

CARL: The other one, the other song I remember. "The Poor Lambs," the "Whiffenpoof Song." That "Baa, Baa, Baa . . ."

ALEX: *(Overlap)* Oh, God, yes.

MARY: Yes, yes—that's my favorite.

GABRIELLE: *(sings)*
Gentlemen songsters off . . .

*(Others haltingly join in)*

GABRIELLE: My God, we even sang that one at Stevens. Where's that from, that's Yale or Harvard . . .

| MARY:<br>It's got to be an Eli . . . | CARL AND ALEX:<br>*(Sing overlap)*<br>We are poor little lambs<br>Who have lost our way |
|---|---|
| GABRIELLE:<br>It invariably made me cry . . . | |

MARY: I love it.

| CARL:<br>All the boys around the piano in about twelve-part harmony. | ALEX:<br>Baa, baa, baa. |
|---|---|

ALEX: Very serious. Camping it up—till we got drunk enough—then really serious.

ALL: *(Sing)*
  Gentlemen songsters . . .

MARY: *(Over)* Oh, but we loved it.

GABRIELLE: Oh, I did too.

ALEX: You should have seen this nut at school. I'll bet
  they were sorry they let him in. Nobody needs a
  quarterback that bad. I mean he was a legend.

CARL: No, I . . .

ALEX: He was, he was a legend. Like Paul Bunyan or
  something. He used to live way the hell out in the
  boondocks. Out of town about a mile from . . .

MARY: Two miles.

ALEX: Way the hell out, halfway to Skokie.

CARL: It kept me in shape.

ALEX: *(Energetically)* Finally he got a car Jun . . .
  what was it, Junior year?

CARL: Sophomore. By Junior I was rooming with you
  and Carson; we were . . .

ALEX: Anyway, Freshman and Sophomore years he's
  out at wherever the hell it was, and he trots into
  town, jogs into town in sweatpants.

MARY: Destroying all the girls right and left.

ALEX: Like hell; he looked deranged.

MARY: Yeah, with his dong flopping around in those sack pants.

ALEX: You wouldn't know him. He looked wild. He wasn't a pussy cat like he is now . . .

CARL: I wasn't any different.

ALEX: *(Without pause)* You . . . He looked deranged. And he runs—sprints into town and this is legend— he's busting toward town and this car pulls alongside of him . . .

MARY: Oh, God.

ALEX: Driving along, Carl doesn't slow down and the guy asks if he can give Carl a lift into town, into the field, and Carl says, "No thanks, I'm in a hurry!"

MARY: *(Over Alex)* Hurry!

*(All laugh)*

CARL: Well, I was; I wasn't even thinking.

ALEX: I mean he was a character! Senior year he nearly wrecked our academic career. Carson and I used to sneak into the room at about four a.m. trying not to wake up Bozo here or turn on any lights and we'd go sprawling over a clothesline this guy's strung across the room. Waist high. But not as a joke. For real. To hang clothes on. I spent half the year on the floor tangled up in his goddamned wet jerseys and sweat socks. Look at him, you know it's true.

*(Carl is grinning. He follows the conversation but stands; the others are seated, a bit off from them)*

CARL: I never knew what time you were . . .

ALEX: *(To Mary)* Well, I don't have to tell you what it was like.

CARL: No, she controlled me pretty . . .

MARY: It was different, though. I only dated him a couple of times before he decided the army needed him. It was incredible. I didn't know what to think. He used to come to me with shoe polish on his cuffs, smelling like a boot-black—and he'd always had a couple of drinks to steel his nerve. He was the returning star and I was the returning homecoming queen. All very lauded over, though they couldn't see allowing us to live in the fraternity house.

GABRIELLE: With his wife, I guess not.

MARY: Not wife . . .

ALEX: Concubine.

Peter Weller, Dianne Wiest

Peter Weller, Dianne Wiest

Jimmie Ray Weeks, Lindsay Crouse

Dianne Wiest, Lindsay Crouse

PHOTOS BY STEPHANIE SAL

MARY: Paramour. Total scandal. And of course Mom, who's more conservative than . . . well, you know . . . was ready to disinherit me.

GABRIELLE: Oh, God, no. All that Wedgewood.

*(Carl crosses to the bar, makes himself another drink)*

MARY: Exactly, almost an ultimatum—the carpets or Carl. No, the wife came afterwards. Everyone was greatly relieved. This is when people still pretended to be moral, you understand. They celebrated for days.

ALEX: We celebrated for nights.

MARY: We really had a neat little house.

CARL: It was cozy. It was cozy.

MARY: It was small. And with drainpipes that made disconcerting digestive noises all night and a fireplace you could have built a closet in. But not a fire, unfortunately.

GABRIELLE: Of course.

MARY: And we did not "have" to get married.

CARL: Not at all, not at all. Ellen was two years yet.

MARY: I just held out as long as I could.

CARL: Yeah? Yeah? I thought you just finally saw the light. Then we bought a little travel agency . . .

MARY: Mom's wedding present.

ALEX: And then a little motel, and then a little shopping center . . .

GABRIELLE: And then a little subdivision.

CARL: It was something else living with this chick. I'd never seen anything so clean. Not just the house, but I used to come home, walk in the door, and the place smelled of . . . not perfume . . . but powder—nothing smells that clean. Used to blow my mind.

MARY: It was very special. Carl was thinner, firmer then. Hard as a wall. And really agile, for his weight, and eager. We made love after he studied till midnight. And then . . . sleeping so close and warm, we used to wake up just as it got light out . . .

CARL: *(Gently)* Summertime; summer term.

MARY: . . . and go at it all over again. I'd fall back asleep, curled up against his chest with his sweaty-wet face at my ear murmuring, "Marry me, Mary, marry me, Mary, marry me . . ." *(Distantly musing)* I don't actually think . . . that I loved him then. But I love him then now.

ALEX: I ran into Carson about a month ago.

MARY: That was their roommate.

ALEX: We had dinner. He's living in Philadelphia. He has four kids. He weighs three hundred pounds. Spent the whole goddamned evening trying to sell me life insurance.

MARY: Well, Alex, with four kids . . .

ALEX: The team could have used you when you went back too.

CARL: Naw, naw, they could have had a good team that year.

ALEX: Yeah, except for Hanesfield as wide receiver. Guy had hands of margarine. And if you think Burns . . .

CARL:
Yeah, well, maybe they could have used a . . .

MARY:
What's wrong, darling?

ALEX:
Yeah, yeah, yeah, yeah.

GABRIELLE:
What? Nothing.

CARL:
They asked! They tried to get me coaching or something. I couldn't cut it. I used to go out and pass a few with them.

MARY:
Silly.

GABRIELLE:
It sounds lovely. I just . . . Oh, God, I'm terrible tonight. I'm just no good at all. Do you get nervous?

ALEX:
Hell, you couldn't . . .

MARY:
God, yes.

CARL:
Anyway, I was getting pretty slow, by then.

GABRIELLE:
. . . I mean all the time . . .

*(The men improvise)*

MARY:
I know *just* what you mean. How come?

GABRIELLE:
Oh, it's just me. I'm incredibly tired lately; I haven't energy for anything. I should take vitamins or something. Eat something.

MARY:
Spinach.

GABRIELLE: Ummmmm.

MARY: Or oysters.

GABRIELLE: Ugh! Thanks, not. I'd prefer being tired.

MARY: That's right, you're the one.

ALEX: How come, doll?

GABRIELLE: Oh, who knows? I thought the movie was depressing. I can't bear the city anymore.

ALEX: You mean after the shops close.

MARY: Well, Washington won't be much improvement.

GABRIELLE: No, there's just too much going on. There's . . .

MARY: Don't let those faggots get to you.

GABRIELLE: It isn't just that. There're just too many people in the world.

ALEX: You're just upset about the demonstration.

GABRIELLE: That was not a demonstration. That was a carousal.

MARY: Demonstration of life-style, maybe.

GABRIELLE: I couldn't make out *what* they thought they were doing.

ALEX: I tried to tell you; you weren't interested.

GABRIELLE: No, and I'm still not; I don't care.

MARY: Nor do they.

GABRIELLE: You try to just drive into town for a perfectly simple evening—

ALEX: At a skin flick?

GABRIELLE: In any case.

MARY: Decidedly disappointing, by the way.

ALEX: For the girls maybe.

MARY: I never felt so overdressed in my life!

GABRIELLE: In any case, to be held up by students—or I don't even know if they were students—swarming all over the street in beards and glitter and eight-hundred-dollar Loden coats.

ALEX: They didn't do a thing, they did no damage—they held up traffic.

GABRIELLE: And to aggravate matters, I thought you were going to get out of the car and join them, you almost . . .

ALEX: They were only having fun; they didn't threaten you, Gabby.

GABRIELLE: The reincarnation of Siegfried himself—they did, they knew it made the people in the cars uptight.

ALEX: *(To Gabrielle)* Well, now whose fault is that, is that their . . . ?

GABRIELLE: It just didn't seem like the most propitious time to announce a political career.

ALEX: If it were a question of announcing it, I can't think of . . .

MARY: They weren't so bad.

GABRIELLE: *(Over)* Oh, I know, I'm wrong. I'm wrong. It's perfectly all right for them to do as they please— after all, what is it I'm so anxious to protect, who am I kidding? It's just . . . Forgive me, OK? I don't want to see it. If it's all the same to everybody.

MARY: They're difficult not to see.

GABRIELLE: I know all the arguments, it's all I ever hear; OK, change it all; I want it to change too—my God, if we're going to be in Washington next year, I'd better have some convictions.

MARY: Not necessarily, from what I hear . . .

GABRIELLE: Only I want to wake up one morning and everything will have been magically accomplished overnight. I'm just not the revolutionary type.

MARY: Me either.

GABRIELLE: I'll go about as far as to sign a petition. *(She sits)*

MARY: I won't even do that. I do nothing. Oh, God, I feel myself more and more becoming an emotional recluse like Mom. Mom walks through her apartment trailing a literal cloud of Jungle Gardenia and two little lilac poodles—Fou Fou and Poo Choo or something—who are continuously high on perfume vapor. And that's her entire life—somehow managing to be elegant, tottering about the apartment trailing the vapors and the two spaced-out poodles, with a cigarette and a glass of white wine in her one hand and a polishing rag in her other. Looking for blurs on her furniture. Fingerprints. She's unbelievable. Ellen, of course, loves her, loves visiting.

GABRIELLE: Real furniture though.

MARY: Oh, God, beautiful. Period Newport, museums are creaming; and about a dozen real Kazaks, a block-front John Townsend chest-on-chest you could die from. And that sustains her. Without interests or friends. I just think the old girl knows something I don't.

ALEX: Or doesn't know something that you . . .

MARY: No, I don't believe that anymore.

GABRIELLE: *(Under)* Alex, you wanted to call the service.

MARY: *(Continues, as Alex goes to the phone)* I'm getting so mean and small and insular—oh, well, it's unimportant, I suppse we all are . . .

ALEX: *(At the phone)* What, what?

MARY: Oh, I just have no patience with people—anyone in the least different from us. And I don't mean importantly or socially, I mean in the pettiest possible sense. Example: I drink coffee black, have all my life —I'm really getting deeply intolerant of people putting cream and sugar in their . . . I sit there watching them measure and dribble and stir and clink and drip their spoon and smile—I really just have no patience with them at all. You put together a dinner party for eight which should be perfectly simple, and Rosie tells you Marvin doesn't eat lamb or Sandy breaks out from chocolate—then leave! Go away. I don't want to know you. I am utterly unconcerned with the person who likes okra.

ALEX: What you're saying is you're this very selfish, very spoiled little girl.

MARY: Oh, come on; well, yes, of course, but you know you feel the same.

ALEX: No, I really don't think so.

MARY: I have a private theory that we're all like that. We all. Our generation. The older generation is . . .

GABRIELLE: Older.

MARY: Older. And the younger . . . well, those I don't understand at all. I think I might admire them tremendously, but . . .

ALEX: Absolutely.

MARY: I'm quite sure—no, not absolutely, I *think*. But I'm quite sure I don't understand them at all. They're so bright and so damn dull all at once. See, I think of the kids and I feel like Mom; I think of Mom and I feel like the kids.

ALEX: Oh, no, Mary, no . . .

MARY: *(Putting her cigarette out)* Why are you always so pig-headed? I'm trying to teach you something.

ALEX: It's just a question of do you want to align yourself with the past or with the future.

MARY: Tell me about the future, and I'll let you know.

ALEX: I'll tell you about the past. The kids today know this. We were silly to quit swinging from the fruit-laden trees and start growing wheat. But wheat makes cake and cake is good and that's rationalization.

MARY: I think you sound like a shoo-in for the under-eighteen vote. Which reminds me, you need a haircut; I've been meaning to tell you all night.

ALEX: That's all Gabby says to me. Mom too.

GABRIELLE: I don't think your mother would vote for him.

MARY: I don't think Mom knows women have the right.

ALEX: Of course I'd like to have got out of the car and gone with those kids.

MARY: *(All overlapping a bit here)* . . . I don't see Alex as the firebrand of social . . .

GABRIELLE: *(Over)* Alex.

ALEX: It's what I feel. With their awareness of what the hell is happening on this planet—I'd give anything to be seventeen now. Eighteen.

GABRIELLE: I wouldn't, thanks.

MARY: Oh, well, Alex, love, darling! That's a whole different thing altogether. *(To Gabrielle)* I wouldn't either; I had acne and no breasts at all. Let me pour another round and we'll *(She rises, collects the glasses)* toast Ponce de León and Alex can lead us in a prayer for world harmony.

ALEX: Carl had better do that; I'm a bit out of the praying habit.

GABRIELLE: None for me, darling.

MARY: Right, darling, with your Sunday School experiences.

CARL: Hmm?

MARY: Carl is three sheets to the wind.

CARL: *(To Mary)* Am I?

MARY: You are. Blistered.

CARL: I never know. No one can tell except Mary. I stopped arguing when I passed out mid-sentence once. Do I what?

*(They laugh)*

CARL: I'm a good drunk.

*(They laugh)*

MARY: Superlative, darling!

ALEX: Pray.

MARY: *(She crosses to the dining room, getting more drinks)* Pray.

CARL: Pray? Ah . . . yes.

ALEX: Seriously.

CARL: No, I do, I do.

ALEX: When?

CARL: Every night. Before I go to sleep. Part of my sleep ritual.

ALEX: Every blessed . . .

CARL: Every night, yes; nearly every night.

ALEX: What do you say, "Now I lay me down to sleep"?

CARL: Uh. Yes. *(Beat)* I'd as soon not discuss it.

ALEX: At least not drunk.

GABRIELLE: Especially not . . .

CARL: I'm not what you'd call terribly religious. I've only been terribly religious once. I mean, like everybody else who sits up for the last late show—I jump up to turn off the sermonette . . .

ALEX: Yeah, before the rabbi from the Cicero precinct can tell me I'm not saved.

CARL: But when I was thirteen, Mom had an operation. I don't think it was serious but operations scare the hell out of me anyway. And this was for . . . well, I won't guess, minor in any case. And I became the most zealously religious little boy in town. I prayed and cried and bartered with God—I promised to quit smoking—I'd been smoking already about three years by then—and to never again masturbate. And never swear if He would spare Mom's life.

GABRIELLE: Oh God.

CARL: And when she recovered . . . quite easily . . . I was positive it was a direct result of my prayers.

GABRIELLE: Absolutely.

CARL: Dreamed of being canonized—we were Baptist, remember—

MARY: Nevertheless.

CARL: I only broke my promise gradually, so I wouldn't notice.

ALEX: Or so God wouldn't notice.

CARL: I didn't actually buy a pack of cigarettes for over a year. By then I had managed to convince myself that she would have recovered anyway. *(He crosses to the sofa, gets a glass. Then he crosses to the desk, looking for a cigarette)* It's very odd. About prayer. I don't quit because I've got all this time invested in it. When the sky suddenly splits wide open one day and angels sing—you look up and say—thank God, I kept up my praying. *(He crosses to the dining room. Beat. He continues, not too seriously, but down)* But I don't think . . . a paradox here. I don't think I ever quite forgave Mom for causing me to make a solemn promise I wasn't strong enough to keep. *(Checking for cigarettes)* Seventeen? No . . .

ALEX: Well, seventeen, eighteen.

CARL: No, no, no, no.

*(Carl finds a cigarette, handing one to Alex)*

ALEX: *(Rubbing his leg)* No, I'm trying to stop.

CARL: *(Looking for matches)* Yeah?

MARY: *(She gives a drink to Alex, Carl, then sits)* Congratulations.

ALEX: Thank you. All of the twelve hours so far. I'll probably just gain weight. Oh, well, it occurred to me I've been intending to quit for the past five years. No joke. For five years, every week I think I'll save some money and buy a carton of cigarettes; then I think, well, hell, I'm giving them up, I'll have quit before I could smoke them all anyway.

*(Carl looks at his watch)*

GABRIELLE: Darling, it's one-thirty.

ALEX: *(Standing, pressing his hand to his leg)* Yeah, well . . .

*(Mary and Gabrielle cross to the hall closet)*

CARL: Your legs?

ALEX: Huh? Oh, yeah.

CARL: Need exercise.

ALEX: No, no. I don't know what it is. Maybe it's just smoking. *(Picking up his coat)* Well.

*(Carl follows)*

GABRIELLE: *(Getting up, taking her coat, a very smart, quite new fur)* Oh, yes. Call tomorrow.

MARY: I'm so glad you got that coat.

GABRIELLE: I'll need it this winter if this is any indication.

ALEX: *(Lines overlap from here to their exit)* Carl, don't forget the game.

CARL: No, I can't watch the team they have now lose.

ALEX: You'll change your mind.

*(They are near the door)*

GABRIELLE: Oh, Alex. Oh, look, it's trick or treat.

MARY: Isn't it ghastly?

CARL: I told you we cleaned up.

MARY: It's all stuck together in one lump.

GABRIELLE: Oh, no, I haven't seen candy corn since I was about twelve.

MARY: It's precious to Ellie. She wanted it in her room, but I convinced her to "share" it with us so she doesn't gorge herself. *(Opening the door)* Brrrrr. It's cold. It's Christmas soon.

ALEX: Oh, don't mention it.

GABRIELLE: Oh, I love it.

ALEX: She's had her Christmas.

MARY: Of course, with Ellen; I love it too.

GABRIELLE: She's just at that age.

ALEX: Yeah, and Carl would make a great Santa Claus.

CARL: Oh, yeah. *(He wanders back into the living room, still in his topcoat with the collar turned up. He sits on the sofa)* Ho, ho, ho!

MARY: I love Christmas out here. And all the carolers; it's beautiful.

ALEX: So does she.

GABRIELLE: I do. *(Singing)* "God rest ye merry gentlemen:

*(Mary joins her)*

| GABRIELLE AND MARY: | ALEX: *(Over)* |
|---|---|
| Let nothing you dismay. | Ring-a-ding |
| Remember  Christ  our | |

Savior was born on
Christmas Day."

MARY: With their bells ringing.

GABRIELLE: *(Overlapping)* And they're all bundled
up, freezing.

ALEX: She loves anything.

*(They say goodnight. Mary shuts the door after them)*

MARY: Brrrr. Jesus. *(She crosses to the living room, collects some glasses. Carl pours the last drink from the
pitcher into his glass. Mary collects the remaining
glasses and pitcher)* Poisonous movie, didn't you
think?

CARL: Pretty bad.

MARY: I'll check on Ellie. Will you be in? *(No reaction
from Carl)* Don't bother I'll be right out.

*(Mary exits into the kitchen with the tray)*

CARL: *(Alone onstage, he sings quietly)* "To save us all
from Satan's power when we have gone astray . . ."
*(Beat)* Yes, it's . . . very difficult.

MARY: *(Coming from the kitchen)* Don't you think you
can take your coat off? They've gone.

CARL: Huh? No, I didn't . . .

MARY: I'm kidding. *(She kisses him on the cheek, then turns out one lamp)* Goodnight, love; don't drink any more.

CARL: *(Putting his glass down)* No, no. *(Mary exits up the stairs)* All of which is not the subject. Prayer, praying. Not the question. The question is why, with all the others, am I up watching the friggin' last late show in the first place! Watching the last late show; hearing you slip out of your dress and your slip. And brush against the carpet walking across to the closet. Listening to your breathing—after you're asleep. No, hell; it's all got to break!

*(Carl takes his glass, looks around, turns off another lamp—leaving the stage still quite light. He takes the glass into the dark kitchen. As he exits, a noise is heard at the front door. A key, stomping, etc. Alex enters, followed by Gabrielle. Gabrielle is somewhat more tired. Alex is somewhat more irritable)*

ALEX: Wheew! God. The house smells like someone had pissed in the fireplace.

GABRIELLE: Alex! My God.

ALEX: About a week ago.

*(They are putting their coats away)*

GABRIELLE: Really, that's not necessary. What'd . . . you used to do that?

ALEX: I don't know now if I really did it or just wanted to do it a lot.

GABRIELLE: *(Crossing to the bedroom)* Where's the bed?—I'm exhausted.

ALEX: *(Tensely)* Wait a second! *(Pause)* Did you leave the light on?

GABRIELLE: Huh? Yes, remember?

ALEX: *(Crossing to the living room)* How come?

GABRIELLE: Oh, I don't know. I felt safer. Foil a burglar today.

*(She lies on the sofa)*

ALEX: Well, that's pretty . . .

GABRIELLE: I feel terrible. God, I hated that movie.

ALEX: All right. Enough. I've heard enough about that movie. I guess it wasn't a very good idea.

GABRIELLE: Wonderful idea. Terrible movie. Will you think less of me if I don't bathe?

ALEX: No, I might have to sleep on the sofa.

GABRIELLE: Be my guest. Carl was really belting them down at dinner, wasn't he?

ALEX: Yes, well, he does that, you know.

GABRIELLE: *(Crossing around the sofa, taking off her dress)* Are you coming to sleep? You must be dropping.

ALEX: I'm not all that tired, actually.

GABRIELLE: There's a switch.

ALEX: If I turn in early, you aren't obliged to go to bed too.

GABRIELLE: If I didn't want to, I wouldn't. *(She sits on the back of the sofa)* You want to tuck me in?

ALEX: Yeah, I'll be in.

*(She slips her arms around his neck and kisses him)*

GABRIELLE: Don't get tense, I'm too tired!

ALEX: Tense? What the . . . what are you talking about?

GABRIELLE: *(Crossing to the bedroom)* OK, darling. If I fall asleep, I love you. *(She goes into the bedroom)*

ALEX: Should I take that as a sign? *(He crosses to the hall. In a German accent)* Vos dis passing mine bedtroom door bare-assed naked, huh?

GABRIELLE: *(Off)* It's cold enough for flannel.

ALEX: Der es un old-fashioned fraulein, ya? Dis all goosepimply? Dis all goosepimply in der.

GABRIELLE: *(Off)* Yes. And it's not fräulein, it's frau. Goodnight, love. Brrrr.

*(The light goes out)*

ALEX: Lieblich dassn't vont turked in?

GABRIELLE: *(Off)* No. Go away. And quit talking like that.

ALEX: *(Straight)* That's pretty good—car to bed in sixty seconds flat.

GABRIELLE: *(Off)* I'm falling apart. I don't feel well at all.

ALEX: You sick?

GABRIELLE: *(Off)* Just tired.

ALEX: You want anything?

GABRIELLE: *(Off)* No, I'm fine.

ALEX: The radio won't bother you, will it?

GABRIELLE: *(Off)* Not a chance.

ALEX: Good night.

GABRIELLE: *(Off)* Night. I love you.

ALEX: I love you.

GABRIELLE: *(Off)* I love you.

ALEX: *(Mimic)* Go away, close the door already; turn on the radio. Get out.

GABRIELLE: *(Off)* There's an idea.

ALEX: Good night, love.

*(Alex closes the door. He turns entry light off, he crosses to the living room, goes to the radio, turns it on low— finds a lively station, goes to the desk, looks through a drawer, and finds a black-stemmed, white-bowled pipe and a small pouch of tobacco. He packs the pipe and lights it. Then he sits down at the desk, looks to the door, and lifts the phone quietly. He dials very slowly. Eleven numbers. He listens and looks to his watch. He sets the phone back in its cradle, wanders to the living room area, and sits in his chair. He turns off the lamp. The audience can still see Alex.*

*Carl comes in from the kitchen, still in his coat. He bangs his coat in the closet, looks around the room . . . empties an ashtray—something he does not do well or often. He crosses to dining room and sits. There is a noise off in the bedroom. The bed jolts. Gabrielle is getting out of bed)*

GABRIELLE: Ah, ah . . .

*(Alex quickly knocks out the pipe and tucks it into his pocket. He turns on the lamp beside the chair. He gets a few steps toward the door as Gabrielle opens it)*

GABRIELLE: *(She crosses to the foyer, gasping)* Ah—oh, oh . . .

ALEX: *(He turns the radio off, crosses to Gabrielle)* What's wrong? Darling?

GABRIELLE: Are there . . .

ALEX: What? You OK, baby?

GABRIELLE: Are there any . . . oh, no . . . I'm . . .

ALEX: *(Laughing teasingly. He turns the light on)* Hey, what's up? You were dreaming. Sweetie? You were asleep.

GABRIELLE: Oh, sweet Jesus.

ALEX: You OK?

GABRIELLE: *(She crosses to the bedroom)* Yeah. Oh, wow; don't wake me up.

ALEX: No.

GABRIELLE: What are you . . . ?

ALEX: I'll be right in. I'm just trying to relax.

GABRIELLE: How long have I been asleep?

ALEX: About five minutes.

GABRIELLE: *(Groaning)* That's not possible . . .

ALEX: Go sleep. You want me to come?

GABRIELLE: I'm OK. Mmmmm. *(She kisses him. She leaves through the door)*

ALEX: *(Crossing to the door)* Door shut?

GABRIELLE: Yes, darling, please.

ALEX: Goodnight.

*(Alex shuts the door, unconsciously wiping his mouth with the back of his hand. He looks at his watch, goes to the desk and sits. Alex quietly dials the number, listens. Carl sits on his end of the sofa)*

ALEX: *(Re the phone)* Goddamn.

CARL: Who are you calling?

ALEX: A girl.

CARL: Age?

ALEX: Seventeen.

CARL: Relationship?

ALEX: I'm not sure.

CARL: You've had her?

ALEX: No. I take her places.

CARL: The ball game, the movies, the museum, the zoo.

ALEX: The botanical gardens once.

CARL: She studies botany.

ALEX: At the University of Chicago.

CARL: And you're in love with her.

ALEX: Something like that.

CARL: Where is she?

ALEX: I was just wondering.

CARL: *(Glancing at his watch)* It's nearly two.

ALEX: Yeah, I know. Well. *(He hangs up the phone)*

CARL: No, no, no, this has got to break wide open.

ALEX: Do I love her? Yes, I think so. But unfortunately I suspect that love is only a neurosis that people have agreed everyone should have together. No different from acrophobia. It isn't a natural process. Like breathing, or eating, or sex. It's tacked on.

CARL: Swimming isn't natural either, but nobody puts it down.

ALEX: As long as you don't grease up and try to cross channels with it.

CARL: What the hell are you doing with this teenager, anyway?

ALEX: Debbie. It isn't like that.

CARL: It sounds pretty damn sick if you want to . . .

ALEX: Carl, the other guy's business always sounds sick.

CARL: Well, what do you do? Nothing? What are you . . . like her uncle?

ALEX: OK. Fine. Exactly. And she's like my respiratory system. Buddy, I'd as soon not . . .

CARL: Yeah, fine by me, only I'd think . . .

ALEX: Carl, it's like I was never young. I must have been purblind and deaf. I didn't see things. You and I drank and had fun and sang, but I didn't see things. This girl knows things I don't even know yet. She knows how to leave herself alone. She has no allegiance, no priorities—everything is valuable to her—equally. As it comes.

CARL: And that's right?

ALEX: I think it might be.

CARL: Oh God, Alex. Don't you want a family? Don't you want to have kids?

ALEX: Jesus! You always ask me that. Every time . . .

CARL: Yeah, well, what do you always answer?

ALEX: 'Cause what I wanted was . . .

CARL: 'Cause what I wanted most used to be a boy—a son. I would have had fifteen of Ellen to get a boy and loved them every one. No lie—I almost blamed Mary for having a girl. Now, of course, I wouldn't trade her. Funny thing, blame. *(He laughs)* Hell, it's still one hell of a kick that Donald's had three girls in a row . . .

ALEX: The CPA, right?

CARL: I hit on an answer. Ellen. Brought us together. Remarkably. Wonderfully.

ALEX: I'd think she would.

CARL: But it wouldn't work now. Not really.

ALEX: Another kid?

CARL: No, not that. I was thinking something else.

ALEX: I thought you were talking about having a . . .

CARL: No, I was thinking people can be brought together by tragedy. If something happened to Ellen . . .

ALEX: Carl, nothing's going to happen to . . .

CARL: But if something did . . . I always wondered what very, very primitive people . . . There's something . . . in . . . it's a fantasy. All in the air. It's all a house of cards. One fantasy . . . lie—balanced on two others. I love them, too.

ALEX: Too damn much.

MARY: *(She enters from Ellie's room, and speaks to a very preoccupied Carl)* I'm sorry, darling. I got embroiled in a drunken question-and-answer session. She went back to sleep. Ellen takes more and more after you—she lacks all coherence. What do you make of Alex's career?

CARL: Has he decided?

MARY: Impending then. I can't decide if he isn't just seeing himself carrying a charger, advancing into battle—in which case . . .

CARL: Honey, you don't carry a charger into battle— the charger is the horse.

MARY: I thought you carried a charger—like a lance. Well, that makes sense. Right then. Charging in *à cheval*—with plumes.

CARL: He might fool us.

*(Alex crosses to the desk, sits)*

MARY: If he's not political, he'll be eaten alive, and if he is political, then I've no interest in him. Why the hell doesn't he just quit and go to work for the Civil Liberties Union if he has such an overpowering social conscience? I know Gabby's confused . . .

CARL: I'd think so. *(As Mary starts to go)* You know I had to make a lot of quick telephone confirmations and I knocked them off this afternoon in about ten minutes flat.

MARY: Good.

CARL: And without even skipping a beat I called Donald and asked him how about knocking it off with my wife.

*(Freeze. A long pause. Alex dials a number, looks at his watch)*

MARY: And what did he say?

CARL: I wasn't even sure I could call him; I didn't actually know I was going to till I hung up.

MARY: Whatever gave you the idea there was anything to knock off?

CARL: No, we won't do that . . .

MARY: Won't do what?

CARL: Pretend. We won't pretend. Of course I'd know. I've known for months. Every Wednesday.

MARY: You're being awfully circuitious for someone with a degree . . .

CARL: No, Mary . . .

MARY: I go into town. I've been seeing Mom almost every week . . . she's no Spring . . .

CARL: I'm not talking about your mother.

MARY: Well, then I haven't . . .

CARL: No, Mary, don't, Mary. I go by the apartment at the Commodore every Wednesday afternoon to check and see if he's showed up. To watch the blinds turn. You turn them up and he turns them down. I told you I'd been spending lunch hours around the Hancock Building and you never even heard me. Doubtless your mind was somewhere else; we know how one-tracked you get. We won't pretend.

MARY: When was that?

CARL: Months ago . . . three months at least; I don't know when.

MARY: Well, why on earth didn't you say something?

CARL: I didn't know . . . *(Alex hangs up. Carl looks to him and back)* . . . what to say. And I kept thinking it'd break off; you'd give it up.

MARY: When did . . .

CARL: I did try. I wrote it out once at work, what I'd say.

MARY: My God, you poor darling . . .

CARL: Oh, come on now.

MARY: No, Carl, if . . .

CARL: Mary, goddamn it, I do not intend to discuss this rationally! I'll be damned if I will. You said what did he say. He said sure, OK, fine, and rather briefly, and I hung up. And thought. Quite a lot. I thought I'm twice again his size. I am. I'm about twice the man's size. I could beat the shit out of the guy and you. And that might make me feel a little better. I'd tell Ellen Mommy fell down the stairs. *(Beat)* I just assumed, whatever he felt about you, that you managed to be in love and that it'd pass . . .

MARY: Oh, God, Carl, couldn't I have seen him just because . . .

CARL: No, I don't like "seen." That's too easy. Say "fucked," say—

MARY: All right, then, just because I got off on it? Without dragging romance through it? Because I dug him?

CARL: OK, it was hot stuff—better than—

MARY: My responsibility to you hasn't altered in the least.

CARL: Yeah, yeah, and Ellen, I know, I know, I know, with all this great guilt we should be even closer now; hell, I guess I should thank him, huh? You must think you married someone else, 'cause I don't work that way. The only thing you can tell me is that it never happened. And how in hell are you going to make it never have happened, huh? How am I going to believe that? None of it happened. The bowl didn't crack, the wheel wasn't bent, the bough didn't break, the cradle didn't fall. You tell me how you're going to tell me that.

MARY: I can't. I wouldn't want to.

CARL: Then goddamnit, Mary, at least you tell me you love the son-of-a-bitch.

MARY: I don't. *(Brief pause)*

ALEX: Jesus, God, you add it all up and I don't understand any of it! The farthest star is several billion light years away on the edge of the universe—beyond which is nothing, Einstein tells us. Not even cold empty space. Nothing. Tricky. Now what is that supposed to mean to me? I have to assume that the Earth and her people might at any moment jump its track and catapult us cold and wet—frosty—into a neighboring solar system—and how stupid, preoccupied, and foolish we'll look. Some embarrassingly superior being will frown questioningly and say, "What do you make of all these facts you present me with?" And we'll say, well, we're working on it. Give us another week. "You mean there are people who are hungry and cold and ten percent of your population controls ninety percent of your food and blankets?" Well, we're working on it. But, we're not. We'll do anything except admit that what we've got here is not just a simple problem of distribution. But recently I read a report from the good old government—why I want to be a part of that, I'll never know—that said we (meaning man) have discovered (meaning America, probably), have discovered just about all there is to know. The mind of man has encompassed most all knowledge, and from now on—however far that may be—we will just be in the process of refinement. That's our future. Sandpapering. Where is the man who wrote that living? When is he living? How would that asshole address himself to the complexity of the human being? To, for instance, that horrible moment when I feel I, myself, just might, one of these deranged and silvery mornings, become that monster you read about who slays his family and himself or fifteen strangers holed up in a tower somewhere . . . come foaming into the breakfast table with your tie awry and your hair uncombed. *(Gabrielle enters, dressed in a neat suit. She hangs her coat in the closet, stands and watches Alex)* Moments all the worse because they are recurrent at the most unguarded times when that prospect, however hideous, is very real. In the middle of culminating a particularly successful business deal or relaxing on the beach in the clean salt air, you still feel it way down deep in your nature somewhere. "Well, tonight, God help me, I may just run completely amok with a meat cleaver." *(Alex finishes in a position—arm over his head or some arrested gesture—then turns to see Gabrielle)*

GABRIELLE: *(Evenly)* Who's Debbie Watkins?

ALEX: *(The gesture remains arrested. Pause)* I don't know.

GABRIELLE: I think if you'd have said almost anything else I'd have thought it was a lie.

*(A long pause)*

ALEX: Your . . . mysterious . . . man caught up with you.

GABRIELLE: Umm. Her father. I was shown what I was told was a rather unflattering photograph of her.

ALEX: A girl. Student. She goes to the University of Chicago.

GABRIELLE: Well I wish we could bring her out here so I could tear the bitch . . .

ALEX: Gabby. I have never . . . believe me; I've never . . .

GABRIELLE: Touched her! Had her! Told her of my love! Pawed her in the back seat of the car! Caressed her hair? What? What the hell are you doing with a girl that age?

ALEX: *(The line is lost under her)* There were none of the ordinary . . .

GABRIELLE: *(As Alex starts to say something)* Honey! Seventeen? Innocent and fragile. Some little candy-licking, anarchist, amoral teenybopper? Taking her to all . . . all our places? Oh, I know how innocent it is; you don't have to tell me. Do you advise them on protest procedures? Aren't you on the wrong side of the . . . aren't you at all curious where she's been for the last four days? She wouldn't bother getting in touch with you because she doesn't even know what fantasies fly around in your mind, does she? Right, Carl—fantasies on fantasies. When I think of the PAIN! Her dad—who is a singularly repellent man . . . I wonder she isn't in a convent—has yanked her out of the University of Chicago and off to her mother in Honolulu. *(Hard beat)* So it's over! Aloha! Is there someone else? IN DESPERATION I asked you. No, no, of course not. I'm just temporarily off you—off sex and the world—I have important decisions to make about our lives. Off sex. What, do you run into the bathroom with a wet towel and—I don't know how these things are done alone, in private—whispering her name—Debbie, Debbie, Debbie, over and over . . . *(Alex takes a step or two toward her)* You touch me and I swear . . .

ALEX: *(After a pause. Rationally)* My relationship with Debbie . . .

GABRIELLE: You didn't have one. Excuse me, lie, I want to hear it. I'm only sorry to intrude into your bleeding heart with my tirade.

ALEX: You know me pretty . . .

GABRIELLE: Well enough to know now nothing I've said has meant a thing. You're pounding all over with your loss—planning a way to get to Honolulu . . .

ALEX: No, not that . . .

GABRIELLE: You're damned right. She wouldn't know what you were doing there. Would she?

ALEX: I don't flatter myself she'd have allowed me to make a pass at her . . . She has . . . friends . . . she didn't pretend to be innocent . . . her father doesn't know her at all.

GABRIELLE: I don't mean she's a virgin; nobody's a virgin anymore. I mean she doesn't know anything about how people work. She didn't know she was getting your rocks off for . . .

ALEX: Maybe she did. I feel she . . . knew what she was doing.

GABRIELLE: Tell me how it works, Alex; is it vicarious gratification . . . voyeurism? I'm slow.

ALEX: All right, you hate this kind of scene, you . . .

GABRIELLE: I love it! Are you kidding! I love it. I'm sick of questioning myself. No more. Pleading. I'm sorry, but my knees are sore. Apologizing. Don't wait up. By God, I was damn near sitting home looming tapestries! Blind! Blind! Blind!

ALEX: *(After a pause. Calm)* I knew when you mentioned him who he was . . . and I've never met the man. I don't know why he followed you.

GABRIELLE: *(Musing)* I told him at first you'd have no way of meeting a girl that age.

ALEX: I had to go to the botanical gardens to see if . . .

GABRIELLE: I'm aware now.

ALEX: She wants to study botany. She was there; showed me around.

GABRIELLE: And you returned the . . .

ALEX: *(Lost, after a pause)* Oh, dear.

GABRIELLE: *(Crossing to the window seat. Furious again at nothing)* Botany. She. Must. Be. *Agog*. In Hawaii!

ALEX: *(Low, miles away)* I'm sure she is.

GABRIELLE: Humm. I thought when the sex started slacking off and constant attention waned we had reached a marvelously settled plateau. I felt married. Jesus! What a swinger! And I suppose that's where you were always able to get pot too, isn't it?

ALEX: Yes.

GABRIELLE: I'd think a man of the world should know better than to fall for his connection.

ALEX: Well, if I have fallen for her—and I see no reason why I shouldn't call it that . . .

MARY: Only a neurosis we've all agreed to have together, like acrophobia, didn't you say?

ALEX: It's all very easy to have perfect vision of the other fellow's failings. Carl says you never felt for . . .

MARY: *(To Alex)* In the way he means—last-ditch desperation—he's probably right. That isn't love, it's self-sacrifice—feeding your life into someone else's veins—whoever can bear to accept it anyway?

CARL: You didn't think of Ellen or me or . . .

MARY: Don't ask questions. I'll only answer . . . my defenses are always down when they should be up and up when they should be down. Do I love Carl? I ache for him. I worry, I pray I won't hurt him; I'll spend my life trying to convince him that I do, rather than hurt him. Isn't that enough?

CARL: You love me?

MARY: Yes.

CARL: Because you're my life.

MARY: I know.

CARL: I never have loved anyone else.

MARY: I know.

CARL: All my life.

MARY: I know.

CARL: Before I knew you.

MARY: I know, darling.

CARL: All my life! Since I was a kid. I was a hero in school and all I wanted, Mary. Everything! Nothing meant anything, nothing was of value to me! In myself! A home, any accomplishment, achievement, position! Morality! Respect! Nothing was of value if I couldn't lay it at a woman's feet some day as a sacrifice, a pledge! The value of everything was in what it meant to you! Now, you better tell me I've built my life on solid rock. It was never a game.

MARY: I know.

CARL: Don't answer me, help me, marry me, Mary. Marry me, Mary; marry me, Mary. Tell me, I vow. Say, I vow.

MARY: Anything, what?

CARL: Say I marry you, to have and to hold, to honor and obey, to love and to cherish, forsaking all others, till death do us part. Tell me we can have it back the way it was.

MARY: I couldn't do that, Carl. *(Pause)* Carl . . . *(Pause)*

CARL: I think the lady had better come into my chamber. *(Beat)* OK, Mary?

MARY: Well don't ask, silly.

*(She goes into the bedroom. He follows, closing the door behind him)*

ALEX: *(After a beat)* I'm beat. Gabrielle, I wonder if I can say it. In my mind. Not always, but often enough, I've had an image of myself with someone. Some ideal. It hasn't been anyone specific—not Debbie really and not you—some girl, image, who moved exactly as I wanted—corresponded with my every move exactly, which I guess is pretty easy in a fantasy. And anything that strengthened our marriage—any real commitment I've resisted. Because I couldn't allow myself to become tied. I've said yes, when everything in my mind said no, resist, it isn't your dream. It isn't your life. Not yet. I know what you must have felt, fighting against something like that. But I've had it. I can't take it. I can't keep lying. It's wearing me out. I've felt constricted, checked at every corner. Maybe I'm someone who shouldn't have been married, not when we were. Maybe it's been binding me just when I had to have my options open, but I can't imagine not having you with me now. Everything is popping for us; maybe it's right that this happened. There's got to be a way we can give each other what we need and take advantage of what's happening here. Maybe we can take this opportunity, go to Washington, start clean, understand each other, giving each other some room. I don't want to stay out here in this wilderness. And we'll try to help . . . the people who need us. *(Off, in the bedroom, there is a loud pistol shot)* I think we can do something. Gabby? Maybe we can do that. Can we do that? Finally?

GABRIELLE: You really are a shit.

ALEX: I'm a shit, I'm a shit; I said it, I don't care. I don't want to lose you and I want us to work together. I happen to think we can do something great. We can fly if we only do it.

GABRIELLE: Well, there's time enough, Alex. Who could think now?

ALEX: You know there isn't. There's no time. The nomination has to be made. It's ours if we say yes.

GABRIELLE: Then no, Alex. I mean yes, for you; it's what you want and I'm glad for you, but it isn't what I want. Not a bit of it. Not at all. I want a home, and children, and love . . .

ALEX: We can have all that and still—

GABRIELLE: And I don't want to help anyone. I'd—in the first place—never be able to convince myself I wasn't helping someone to make myself feel noble, and I'd feel better making myself feel noble honestly.

*(The phone rings)*

ALEX: Oh, Jesus.

GABRIELLE: The service will get it.

ALEX: *(Answering the phone)* Hello.

*(Carl enters, cradling the telephone at his ear, fumbling with a pistol in his hand)*

CARL: Al? Alex? Hey, meathead! This you?

ALEX: Christ. It's Carl.

CARL: Hell, I didn't recognize your voice. *(This is all very rapid and almost without pause to listen)* Baby, I tell you. I am the prize hamburger! Well, what do you think? Listen, we talked it over; we sat down like two human beings for a change and . . . well of course! Hell, she didn't feel anything about that guy . . . man, I mean the guy's half my size!

ALEX: What did I tell you . . . ?

CARL: *(Laughing)* Yeah, yeah, yeah; right, right, right . . . Hell, he must know himself 'cause Mary can't fake it! Alex, it's great! Now listen . . .

*(Carl holds the phone away for a second, gasping for breath. A look of intense pain is on his face)*

ALEX: Carl?

CARL: *(The happy look is forced back as he speaks again)* Now, listen, you're going to understand this— you know that place up at Lake Elizabeth? Well, we're going to drive up there, the three of us tonight. And . . .

ALEX: I thought . . .

CARL: No. We're leaving right now, Buddy . . . I just want to *(He is breaking down, but he keeps trying)* tell you and thank you for listening to all my . . .

ALEX: No.

CARL: I know! What it must have been! Yeah! *(The laughter becomes blubbering, almost incoherent. Carl is still trying to speak jovially)* Alex, Alex, she's got a hold of my elbow, boy. We're leaving right this minute. I just wanted you to know so you wouldn't worry. All right, boy? Huh?

ALEX: Sure.

CARL: *(Breaking down completely)* Listen, you take care of yourself, you hear? Old Buddy? Huh? Old Buddy?

ALEX: Sure. You OK?

CARL: I'm OK. I'm OK. You be good, Buddy! *(Still nodding, crying, Carl drops the phone, goes up the stairs)*

ALEX: Hey Bozo?

*(After a moment Alex hangs up. Gabrielle goes into the bedroom)*

ALEX: Gabby, did you tell me Carl and Mary sold that house on the lake? *(Alex stands frozen. Grabbing up his coat, he runs out)* Oh God! Oh God!

*(Gabrielle comes from the bedroom with an overnight case. She stands in the middle of the foyer)*

ALEX: *(Offstage. Pounding on the back door. Ringing the back bell)* Carl? Bozo? *(Sounds of a window be-*

*ing broken in the kitchen. Alex runs in)* Mary? Carl?
*(Gunshot offstage)* Ellen? Carl? *(Gunshot offstage)*

*(Gabrielle takes a cloth coat from the front closet and
goes out the front door. Alex turns toward the sound of
her leaving)*

*(Curtain)*